FORTY YEARS A LEGISLATOR

A member of the U.S. Congress from March 1923 to January 1951, Elmer Thomas served two terms in the House and four terms in the Senate. This photo, likely taken in the early 1920s, was used in all four of his Senate campaigns. Courtesy Carl Albert Center Congressional Archives, University of Oklahoma.

Forty Years a Legislator

ELMER THOMAS

Edited by Richard Lowitt and Carolyn G. Hanneman

Foreword by Cindy Simon Rosenthal

University of Oklahoma Press : Norman

Library of Congress Cataloging-in-Publication Data
Thomas, Elmer, 1876–1965.
Forty years a legislator / by Elmer Thomas ; edited by Richard Lowitt and
Carolyn G. Hanneman ; foreword by Cindy Simon Rosenthal. — 1st ed.
p. cm.
Includes index.
ISBN 978-0-8061-3809-1 (hardcover) ISBN 978-0-8061-9493-6 (paper)
1. Thomas, Elmer, 1876–1965. 2. Legislators—United States—Biography.
3. United States. Congress. Senate—Biography. 4. United States.
Congress. House—Biography. 5. Legislators—Oklahoma—Biography. 6.
United States—Politics and government—1919–1933. 7. United S tates
—Politics and government—1933–1945. 8. United States—Politics and
government—1945–1953. 9. Oklahoma—Politics and government—
1907– I . Lowitt, Richard, 1922– I I. Hanneman, Carolyn G., 1950–
   III. Carl Albert Congressional Research and Studies Center.

Congressional Archives. IV. Title.
E748.T475A3 2007
328.73092 — dc22
[B]   2006025551

The paper in this book meets the guidelines for permanence and
durability of the Committee on Production Guidelines for Book Longevity
of the Council on Library Resources, Inc. ∞

To David L. Boren, United States Senator,
1979–1994

Contents

Illustrations

Foreword

The Carl Albert Congressional Research and Studies Center at the University of Oklahoma offers this edition of John William Elmer Thomas's memoir "Forty Years a Legislator" to celebrate the centennial of the state of Oklahoma. Thomas arrived in Oklahoma at the outset of the twentieth century and quickly involved himself in a career of public service that would ultimately span fifty years. Thomas was active in the public life of Medicine Park, where he was a primary developer, and of Lawton, which became his hometown. He served as a state senator from 1907, when Oklahoma became the forty-sixth state, until 1920. He served two terms in the House of Representatives, and in 1926 was elected to the United States Senate, where he served four terms. His career spans the critical years in which Oklahoma defined itself as a multicultural, largely rural state predicated on the development of its abundant land, water, and mineral resources. Thomas found himself deeply involved in the critical issues enveloping the nation during the years of the Great Depression, World War Two, and the emerging cold war.

Thomas's memoir is drawn from the massive collection of his papers in the archives of the Carl Albert Center, a treasure trove of information on Oklahoma history. The center was established in

1979 by the Oklahoma State Regents for Higher Education and the Board of Regents of the University of Oklahoma as a tribute to the ideals, leadership, and accomplishments of Carl Albert, the forty-sixth Speaker of the U.S. House of Representatives, a Rhodes Scholar, and a graduate of the University of Oklahoma.

The Carl Albert Center brings together scholars, students, and citizens to nurture the values of representative democracy. It offers academic programs at both the undergraduate and graduate levels. The Center promotes the scholarly endeavors of both faculty and students to explore aspects of politics and Congress. It also provides a repository for the papers of over fifty former members of Congress as well as the files of several legislative and political aides, journalists, scholars, and organizations. Finally, the Center fosters a wider appreciation and understanding of Congress through a public outreach program that includes exhibits, lecture series, and publications, such as this memoir.

The Carl Albert Center is proud to be associated with the publication of this volume. I would like to thank Richard Lowitt and Carolyn G. Hanneman for their efforts in bringing Elmer Thomas's interesting and important perspective and insight to the public. The Carl Albert Center shares this work in the hope that it fosters an understanding not only of Senator Thomas's life but more generally of who we are as a state and a nation.

Cindy Simon Rosenthal
Director and Curator
Carl Albert Center

Acknowledgments

As editors, we owe a special thanks to Gary Copeland, past director of the Carl Albert Center, who at the outset encouraged our project and provided the financial support that enabled us to secure a working draft of the manuscript. In addition, we want to express our appreciation to Carol Roberts, then a staff assistant in Document Production at the University of Oklahoma, who performed yeoman service in scanning and retyping our draft of the manuscript and then preparing the completed version. We also want to thank the Oklahoma Publishing Company, which provided us gratis with two photos of Thomas during his first years in Oklahoma. Finally we want to thank Steven Baker and the staff at the University of Oklahoma Press.

Introduction

John William Elmer Thomas was a major figure active in public life during the first half of the twentieth century. He served thirteen years in the Oklahoma Senate, defining guidelines and procedures that launched Oklahoma as the forty-sixth state in the Union. This was followed by two terms in the U.S. House of Representatives. In 1926 he was elected to the first of his four successive terms in the U.S. Senate. He retired from the Senate in January 1951 and shortly thereafter drafted this remembrance, "Forty Years a Legislator." It is now part of the massive collection of his papers on deposit in the Carl Albert Congressional Research and Studies Center at the University of Oklahoma.

Thomas's manuscript memoir is a sprawling, unrevised and uncorrected 433-page typed document. The copy at the Carl Albert Center, completed in July 1954, covers his life up to his retirement in 1951. Contained here are accounts of his legislative concerns, including excerpts from his speeches in Congress as well as talks to various groups of bankers and others, expounding chiefly his monetary views. After reading, then discussing and pondering the voluminous typescript, we concluded that with careful and extensive editing, this large core of historically significant material would illuminate the life and career of Oklahoma's first four-term U.S.

senator and at the same time expand our knowledge and understanding of significant aspects of American history during the first half of the last century. While not providing a survey of political life during his tenure, Thomas's memoir does keenly analyze critical issues, both state and national, that fell within his purview. As a Bryan Democrat he was aware of the marked economic disparities between the individual and the corporation. In Oklahoma that awareness was manifested in his concern for the plight of farmers, working people, and Indians. In his fight for monetary reform, he understood that success depended on convincing not only those sympathetic to his concerns but especially his critics.

His successful challenge to the conventional wisdom on the sanctity of a balanced budget in periods of depression indicates that Thomas was an influential and significant public servant. When he left the Senate, he was outranked by only two of his colleagues. He was twice chairman of the Committee on Agriculture and Forestry and most important to Oklahoma, headed the Committee on Indian Affairs from 1935 to 1944. As the second-ranking member on the Committee on Appropriations, he traveled widely before, during, and after the Second World War, gathering information to assist the Senate in determining the allocation of public funds.

Despite his significance as a prominent Oklahoman—among the most significant in the first half of the twentieth century—Thomas's career has commanded little scholarly attention. In their authoritative study of Oklahoma politics, James Scales and Danney Goble write that Elmer Thomas "has remained one of the least known of Oklahoma's political figures."[1] A dissertation written in the 1950s probed Thomas's concern for both the farm problem and the money issue. His interest in Indian affairs, a topic of importance to every individual in the Oklahoma congressional delegation, has attracted some scholarly interest.

The Thomas collection seems to have suffered the fate of most papers of prominent public servants in recent decades. As American society and culture underwent fundamental changes in the latter half of the twentieth century, scholarly interest shifted as well, focusing on themes and concerns that paid less and less attention to issues that consumed Thomas, his colleagues, and the American people. As Oklahoma enters its second century of statehood and in the hope that this remembrance will bring Elmer Thomas once again some of the public recognition he merits, we are presenting this edition as a contribution of the Carl Albert Center to the centennial celebration of Oklahoma statehood.

In editing the manuscript, we considered Thomas's insertion of lengthy segments of some of his speeches, letters, and congressional reports. He also offered tedious observations on issues and topics that digressed from his public concerns. We have scrupulously edited this material, deleting some sections, eliminating redundancies, and structuring pages of single sentences into meaningful paragraphs. In addition, we have not included the first pages of the manuscript, in which Thomas reviewed his early life in Indiana.

Thomas was born on a farm near Greencastle, Indiana, on September 8, 1876, and attended the elementary and secondary schools of his district before studying law at Central Normal College in Danville, Indiana. Graduating in 1897 and gaining admission to the Indiana bar, Thomas, instead of engaging in a law practice, enrolled at DePauw University, in Greencastle, to pursue a degree in liberal arts. He graduated in 1900 and shortly thereafter moved to Lawton, Oklahoma Territory, where he set up a legal practice and began purchasing real estate. He was primarily responsible for founding and developing the town of Medicine Park, adjacent to the Wichita Mountains Wildlife Reserve, where he made his home until he went to Washington. When Oklahoma entered the Union in 1907, Thomas became one of its first legislators. He chaired the Committee on Appropriations and concerned himself with the means of financing the construction of schools, roads, and state institutions, including the state capitol. We launch our edition of Thomas's manuscript with his ample discussion of his early years in Oklahoma.

In 1920 Thomas resigned his seat in the state senate to seek one in Washington as a member of the House of Representatives. He was defeated, losing to his Republican opponent by less than a thousand votes. He tried again in 1922 and this time was successful, winning the seat of the Sixth Congressional District again in 1924. In Congress he focused on issues similar to many he worked on in the state legislature and expanded his interest in agriculture and Indian affairs.

As a young man in Indiana, Thomas honed his skills as an orator and became an enthusiastic supporter of William Jennings Bryan. It was during the Bryan campaign in 1896 that he became interested in what he called the science of money. An advocate of free silver, Thomas believed that putting more money in circulation would make commodities cheaper and lead to a rise in farm prices. In the House and then in the Senate, Thomas probed the manifold operations of the Federal Reserve System, and as the farm crisis of the 1920s merged into the Great Depression, he consistently argued in favor of inflating the currency to stimulate the economy. Thomas sought to know where funds flowed and how the monetary system worked so that it could be modified and made more equitable. In the 1920s, he developed his views in speeches before various assemblages of bankers and others, and he articulated them during the Herbert Hoover administration before colleagues and Wall Street bankers and on the Capitol steps for members of the Bonus Expeditionary Force. His argument that lowering the dollar's gold content in order to drive up local price levels for the output of farmers and industry ran contrary to the views of the Federal Reserve Board, Wall Street, and most members of the banking community, almost all of whom maintained steadfast adherence to the gold standard and a stabilized economy. He made his greatest con-

tribution in 1933, when he introduced an amendment allowing the
president to adjust the money supply to cheapen the dollar, seeking
in this way to break the hold of deflation. This would thereby allow
prices to rise so as to put cash in the empty pockets of the disadvan-
taged — defined as farmers, wage earners, Native Americans, and
consumers — Thomas's constituents as well as a major portion of
the American population. In a lengthy debate in which he displayed his mastery of the issue, Thomas convinced enough of his
colleagues of the validity of his views. The amendment, incorporated into the farm bill, was crucial to the early success of the New
Deal.

President Franklin D. Roosevelt had previously recalled the
American delegation from the London Conference, where world
leaders considered means of coping with the worldwide economic
collapse through a strict adherence to a gold standard. Recalling
the American delegation meant that the administration would seek
an American response to the depression crisis. The Thomas amendment gave the president authority to promote reflation by de-
stabilizing the currency and thus to help restore commodity price
levels. The administration could also initiate programs to give work
to the unemployed, to make possible the payment of debts closer to
the level at which they were incurred, and to restore more balance
in the price structure so that farmers could exchange their produce
for the products of industry on a fairer basis. The amendment gave
Roosevelt more power over monetary matters than had been extended to any previous president and helped launch the New Deal.

Earlier in 1929, in his first term as a senator, Thomas conducted
one of the most unusual filibusters in American history. Speaking on behalf of Oklahoma oil producers and workers, Thomas
attracted national attention when he brought the Senate to a standstill at the end of the second session of the Seventy-first Congress.
During the debate on the Hawley-Smoot Tariff, which established
the highest rates in American history, Thomas argued for a tariff

on crude oil and incurred the wrath of the bill's supporters who
opposed such a plank. Thanks to Thomas's filibuster, final debate
was postponed until the next session of Congress.

Throughout his manuscript Thomas relates his involvement with
measures and projects that directly improved the lot of his constituents. For example, he helped the Kiowa, Comanche, and Apache
tribes secure control of the oil under the Red River. In addition, he
supported the creation of the only Bureau of Reclamation project
in Oklahoma (near Altus), as well as other water projects, which
changed the quality of life for many of the state's citizens.

With his service on the Committee on Appropriations, Thomas
surveyed the state of the nation's preparedness for war in 1939–
1940 and later assessed the devastation in postwar Europe and the
impact of the Marshall Plan. Particularly interesting is his account
of a visit to Nürnberg, where he attended the final session of the war
crimes trial and toured the prison that housed the defendants.
Especially important was his service on a committee with three
other senators — all pledged to secrecy — who were kept abreast of
the development of nuclear energy. As one of only four senators
entrusted with the biggest and best kept secret of the twentieth
century — the development of the atomic bomb — he also chaired
the Senate Subcommittee on Military Appropriations and, in that
capacity, had to push funding measures through Congress without
disclosing their true nature. Thomas's role and that of the subcommittee, fully related in the memoir and largely unknown to
scholars, adds further insight to an understanding of congressional
relations during the war years.

In the concluding portions of his memoir, Thomas presents an
eloquent argument for seniority in the Senate, a defense that car-
ries little weight today, when many members early in their tenure
secure the chair of a subcommittee, a practice unknown during his
time. Equally impressive is Thomas's lofty statement of the populist
faith that animated his entire political life. He concludes his re-

membrance with a statement by his younger colleague Robert S. Kerr, who delineated Thomas's contributions in promoting the welfare of the people of Oklahoma.

Seeking a fifth term in the U.S. Senate in 1950, Thomas was defeated in the Democratic runoff primary election by A. S. "Mike" Monroney, who later gained the seat. After his public career ended, Thomas practiced law in Washington, drafted this manuscript, and authored *Financial Engineering* and *Autobiography of an Enigma.*[2] He returned to Lawton in 1957 and died at age eighty-nine after surgery on September 19, 1965. In his prime, Thomas was an impressive figure: six feet, two inches tall, erect in carriage, fastidious in dress, serious-minded, and solemn in demeanor. His typically lengthy speeches were delivered in clipped precise words, at times aided by charts, and forcefully presented without rhetorical flourishes. William Jennings Bryan and Thomas's rural Indiana background inculcated in him three themes evident in his career in Oklahoma: land, money, and transportation. When translated into legislation, these ideas could improve the lot of rural residents and working people, whom he regarded as his chief constituents. These themes are reflected throughout "Forty Years a Legislator."

FORTY YEARS A LEGISLATOR

I arrived in Oklahoma City late on Sunday afternoon, November 16, 1900. Heavy rains had fallen and the streams were full and overflowing. There was no paving in Oklahoma City and the mud was so deep that it required four horses to pull the small bus from the Frisco station to the hotel. Little did I think that first night that exactly seven years to a day thereafter the two territories would be admitted to full statehood under the name of "Oklahoma."

GETTING ESTABLISHED IN THE TERRITORY

After a few days of investigation, including a trip into the country with a group of northern homeseekers, for the best of reasons I definitely decided to remain permanently in the Indian country. The all-compelling reason for such decision was the fact that I did not have money enough to pay my car fare back to Indiana.

At that time Oklahoma City claimed to have ten thousand population. The farms adjacent to the city had been homesteaded and many of the settlers were willing and even anxious to sell their lands so that they might return to their former homes in the states. This meant that much farm land was on the market for sale. I soon learned that the real estate business was profitable in Oklahoma City and likewise throughout the entire territory. Railroads were being built in almost every direction. New town sites were being established, and the remainder of the public lands in western Oklahoma was being filed on and the population was increasing rapidly. I did not have finances to participate in the lively speculation; hence, I had to confine my efforts to the practice of law.

One of the first men I met at Oklahoma City was Jay M. Jackson, the head of the Jay M. Jackson Real Estate Company.[1] Mr. Jackson had a number of rooms in a two-story building located on the corner of First and Broadway, and being in need of a lawyer and notary public, he offered to let me have one of his rooms for my law office.

I applied for a license to practice law in the territory and also made application for a commission as a notary public. The board representing the local bar association accepted my credentials in the form of a Certificate of Admission to practice law in Indiana and issued me a license to practice law in Oklahoma Territory. Also my commission as a notary public was as promptly authorized and delivered. Then with the two certificates I opened my law office and hung out my shingle at the foot of the stairs leading up to the Jay M. Jackson real estate office.

The established attorneys had the best of such law business as developed, but the population was increasing rapidly and the newcomers, being interested in securing locations for business and acquiring city property as well as farms, patronized such lawyers as were recommended or visited the first law office they came across. This meant that with such business as came to me from the adjacent real estate office, along with business from transients, I was able to pay expenses and to accumulate some reserves.

In order to extend my acquaintance with the businessmen, I joined the Chamber of Commerce and the contacts made the year I resided in Oklahoma City were of great value to me in later years. All this time, however, I was awaiting the lottery opening of the Indian [lands in southwestern Oklahoma] . . ., such lottery to take place on August 6, 1901. I had planned to participate in the opening in the hope of drawing a lucky number and thus have a chance to secure a valuable tract of land adjacent to or near one of the new county seats to be established. So, while I was making more money than I had ever earned before, when the program for the lottery

When Elmer Thomas first arrived in Oklahoma Territory in 1900, he immediately sought licenses to practice law and to serve as a notary public. He soon realized that he could make money notarizing the necessary registration documents for settlers clamoring for the Indian lands in southwestern Oklahoma that were opened by lottery in 1901. Shortly before this land was opened, Thomas moved his office to Lawton. Thomas is the taller man in the center background. Copyright 1901, The Oklahoma Publishing Company.

was announced I decided to open a temporary office in El Reno to assist applicants in the preparation of their papers necessary for registration.

A tent was erected in the middle of one of the streets; blanks were secured and, being a notary public, on the opening day for registration I was ready for business. Under the rules and regulations the only charge that could be made for preparing registration papers was the 25-cent notarial fee. However, with slight expenses, the daily volume of people interested in the government land lottery made the returns from the middle of the street, open tent registration office very substantial. Those who participated in the Oklahoma land opening in 1901 now remember the buying power of 25 cents in those early days. With a quarter, one could buy a meal almost any place and have some money left.

The registration period lasted only a few days, but during that time both government official registration points—El Reno and Fort Sill—were visited by multiplied thousands of homeseekers. When the registration period was over, the name and address of each registrant was placed on a small card and sealed in a comparably sized envelope. Then a container large enough to hold all the envelopes was made in the shape of a barrel. The barrel was mounted on a frame so that it could be turned over and over, and then the lottery machine was set up on a specially constructed platform high enough so that all interested could witness the drawing.

On the publicly announced day for the drawing, a large crowd assembled. Strong men operated the cranks which caused the barrel containing the envelopes to rotate, and after turning the barrel over backward and forward many times, the official in charge ordered the operation to stop. A young girl, under ten years of age, had been selected and blindfolded to draw from the barrel the first series of envelopes containing the names of the lucky registrants. When all was ready a small door or lid on top of the barrel was opened and the young girl, standing on a chair, reached in the barrel and drew therefrom a single envelope.

The envelope was handed over to the government official in charge of the drawing and by him opened and the name and address of the lucky person was announced to the assembled multitude. The first card drawn was given number "one." This procedure meant that the person whose name was on the card was entitled to have first choice of all the farms or claims, as they were called, located under the jurisdiction of the Lawton land office.

On the first card drawn from the barrel was the name of James R. Woods, a young hardware clerk from Weatherford, Oklahoma, who in selecting his claim filed on a 160-acre tract a quarter of a mile wide and one mile long joining the town site of Lawton on the south. The second card drawn contained the name of Mattie Beal, a telephone operator from Wichita, Kansas, who selected her farm adjoining the Woods claim.

Under the law a homesteader had to actually live on the land for a specified time before being entitled to receive a patent or title from the government. Both Mr. Woods and Miss Beal established residence on their claims, and in due time each made application for and received patents or titles from the United States. As was expected, the moment the patents were received, both had their farms sub-divided into town lots and began to dispose of the property. Thus, through a government-planned and -conducted land lottery, a young hardware clerk and a young working girl from an adjoining state became immensely wealthy in less than one year's time.[2]

LOCATED AT LAWTON

Some have inquired of me as to why I selected Lawton for my home, rather than either Anadarko or Hobart—the other two county seat towns. To me at least, the reason for my choice was clear. During

the so-called Philippine insurrection, in the late nineties, a distinguished Indiana major general by the name of Henry W. Lawton
was killed in operations against Aguinaldo.

Henry W. Lawton, although born in Ohio, moved to Indiana and
served through the Civil War as a private soldier. [He] then was
commissioned as a second lieutenant in the regular Army, 41st
Indiana Infantry, where because of his ability,[he] was given assignments against the Sioux (1876) [and] against the Utes (1879). . . .
In 1886, [his troops] captured Geronimo and his band of Apaches,
but only after a thousand-mile pursuit across Arizona Territory and
Mexico. He was elevated to the rank of major general during the
Spanish American War and, in 1898, was ordered to the Philippines
where, after the capture of Santa Cruz and San Isidro, he was killed
by an insurgent sharpshooter in the line of duty at San Mateo. . . .
The county seat of Kiowa County was named after Garret A. Hobart, then Republican vice-president of the United States, and the
third county seat was given an Indian name — Anadarko; hence,
irrespective of location or future possibilities, I chose to locate at
Lawton in order to pay further respect to a fellow "Hoosier."

I arrived at the Lawton town site on July 29, 1901. The new
country was opened for legal settlement on August 6, 1901, and on
the same day the sale of Lawton town lots by public auction began.
On September 24, 1902, I married Edith Smith, who was born in
Plankington, South Dakota, on June 8, 1884. On September 19,
1904, our first and only child, Wilford Smith Thomas, was born. My
son, known as "Bill," is in business in the town of his birth.

With the opening of the new country, I closed my law office in
Oklahoma City and settled down to practice law at Lawton. The new
county seat town was located immediately adjacent to the Fort Sill
Military Reservation and also at the foot of the Wichita range of
mountains. . . .

On July 29, 1901, when I first reached the bleak prairie tract of
land set aside for the Lawton town site, I learned that there was little

known water in that section of Oklahoma. There were many ravines, branches, and sizeable evidences of streams and even rivers, but at that time all were dry. Cache Creek to the east of the town site was not running, but there was a stagnant pool of water now and then. Medicine Creek, having its source in the Wichita Mountains, was also dry, save a water hole occasionally. Springs were scarce and far between. In the early days of Lawton, all the water to be had was from water wagons which paraded the trails called streets. To secure water from a wagon, a recipient had to provide his own bucket or container.

During the first fall after the opening on August 6th, water was perhaps Lawton's scarcest commodity. It was common for families to boast about how many members could use the same water for bathing purposes. Some contended that they literally wore out the water through excessive use.

The scarcity of water gave me an idea that if a place could be found in the nearby mountains where water could be impounded and made available to the public, that an attractive resort might be developed. With such a project in mind, I began to make a sort of survey of the Wichita Mountain area and in so doing I learned that most of Medicine Creek, which drained much of the mountains, had already been selected by Indians for allotments. Also, the government maps showed that the Fort Sill Military Reservation embraced and protected the balance of the creek. However, a closer survey disclosed that there was one section embracing 640 acres that was neither allotted nor included in the military reserve.

The isolated tract was adjacent to the Wichita Forest Reserve to the west and likewise adjacent to the Fort Sill reservation on the south. The maps showed that Medicine Creek ran through almost the center of the section. With such information I made a personal inspection of the rough mountain land. No road or even trail led to the area, so the inspection had to be made on foot.

The tract was found to be located at the foot and to the southeast of Mt. Scott, the tallest peak of the Wichita range. While there was no water in the creek bed on September 8, 1901, I saw plenty of evidence that much water fell on the mountains and naturally had to flow away down Medicine Creek. My inspection of the area enabled me to locate a number of small dam sites for reservoirs, and then there were two natural dam sites for larger reservoirs or artificial lakes. One of the dam sites was on a portion of the public land which had just been opened for homestead settlement. The second site was on Little Medicine Creek located in the forest reserve about one-fourth mile to the west of the free section which I had located.

While the whole country was devoid of water at that time, yet I knew that there would be plenty of water at times during the year and that if dams were built, there could be developed an abundant supply of pure run-off mountain water. Likewise, knowing that the new county seat town of Lawton would have to locate and develop a water supply, I was convinced that I had located a site not only for a resort but in addition a site for a water supply for Lawton.

With such conviction, I decided to begin to acquire the land. The land office records showed that some of the section had been filed on, but it was obvious that no one could make a living on the land. The records showed further that some of the land was still vacant, so having failed to secure a claim in the government land lottery, I decided to file on 160 acres of the rough mountain land near but not touching Medicine Creek. It developed that all of the main creek had been covered by homestead filings, so my problem was to locate the homesteaders and try to get them to prove up on their claims and then to sell the lands to me for as little consideration as possible. The filings had been made without having first inspected the land, so I did not have much trouble in keeping the land values down. Inasmuch as I did not own the land I could not divulge my plans. As fast as possible, I secured title to the entire section and in doing so I found it advisable to acquire some other rough land on the theory that if my plans failed, the land could still be developed into a cattle ranch.

The dam site on Little Medicine Creek could not be developed at that time, because it was in the forest reserve. The dam site on Medicine Creek proper was secured through a warranty deed from the original homesteader. While I owned the dam site, practically all the land to be covered with water was owned by Indians with allotments. This meant that in order to see the dam built and a large lake constructed, I would have to sell the idea to the Lawton city officials. This task took both work and time. I offered to either sell the dam site to the city or I would barter the site for a perpetual water right. The city officials decided to approve the site for a water supply but would not consider either the purchase or the trade for water. Instead they decided to condemn the property along with the vast amount of Indian land that had to be secured for the reservoir proper. All matters were worked out in time but it was not until July 4, 1908, that I could publicly announce that a town site had been surveyed and that a mountain resort named "Medicine Park" would be opened. In order to build the dam and to transport the materials to the site, the city had to first build a road. Such funds as I could secure had already been used in acquiring the land and in making the necessary surveys.

As I had envisioned, rains came and at times there was an abundance of water coming out of the mountains. It was clear that if dams were built in the narrow granite gorges, there would be impounded a vast supply of good water. The first mountain water supply for Lawton was obtained by laying an 18-inch pipe to the dam site and then building a crude concrete masonry dam about four feet high, in fact just high enough to force the running creek water into the pipe where it was conveyed on to the town many feet below and some 15 miles away. Such plan worked until the first dry spell came and the creek almost went dry again. It did not take much time or argument to convince the city officials that a large dam should be rushed to completion.

The plans for a dam 50 feet in height were soon underway and luckily no great shortage of water was experienced prior to the completion of the project. All during this time the water for Lawton was unfiltered creek water and at times was not of an approved quality. It took World War One, when the Fort Sill reservation became a vast training camp, to secure the construction of a filter plant.

All this time Medicine Park was making progress, but slowly. From the funds secured from Lawton through condemnation of the dam site and adjacent lands and from the sale of cottage sites, two small dams were constructed — one creating a pool for bathing and the other creating a small lake for fishing and boating. Along with the water development a rather large pavilion containing a store, soda fountain, dining room, and kitchen was constructed. Small cottages with screened porches were provided for guests, and tents were provided for campers. Such water as was developed was stocked with game fish, such as bass, crappie, bream, and channel cat.

The fact that there was no other watering place in either southern Oklahoma or northern Texas was responsible for all the patronage that could be accommodated at the rather primitive mountain resort. Within a few years the Park, as it was called, had been improved with a hotel, general store, bath house, dancing pavilion, garage, laundry, post office, some one hundred rock and frame cottages, together with many concessions and departments. In season, beginning about May 1st and ending shortly after Labor Day, the Park population ran around 2,500. The cottage sites sold were improved so that a large part of the summer population became permanent.

The overall development called for improved roads to the Park and improved streets in the resort. Medicine Creek had to be bridged and a school building had to be constructed. The town site was not incorporated, so that all improvements had to be privately financed. This meant that the proceeds from the sale of cottage sites, as well as the profits from all operations, had to be used to pay for the necessary improvements. . . . From the opening of the Park in 1908 to 1922, when I was elected to Congress, I spent considerable time operating the resort and either attending sessions of the State Senate or making improvements in the resort.

The experience gained in operating so many and varied businesses was of great value in my work as a legislator, both in Oklahoma and in Washington. When I was elected to the United States Senate, I realized that I would have to be away from my home almost all the time, so I decided to dispose of all my property and business interests. I found buyers, made deals, and sold everything save the rock house which I had personally planned and constructed, even before I took my seat as a senator. The rock house . . . continued to be my residence during the time I served in the Congress. . . .[3]

Inasmuch as my home is near Lawton, located in almost the center of the Kiowa, Comanche, and Apache Indian [lands] . . ., and because of my legislative work, I came in close contact with the leaders, governors, and chiefs of the several Indian tribes. In the early days . . . Quanah Parker was chief of the Comanches; Lone Wolf was chief of the Kiowas; and Geronimo [chief of the Chiricahua Apaches] was a prisoner of war and confined to the Fort Sill Military Reservation. Through my association with many Indians and their leaders, I soon learned of some of their outstanding traits. Indians, for good reasons, are skeptical of the white man and maintain an air of isolation and aloofness when in the presence of others than members of their own race. This trait causes the Indian to keep his counsel and to await until he is spoken to before talking himself.

The Indian afoot, on horseback, or in wagon will give the white man all the path, sidewalk, or road if he indicates that he wants it,

The Lawton Baseball Club poses in 1904. A lawyer in Lawton, Elmer Thomas served as club manager. He was assisted by Al Jennings, also an attorney. A one-time train robber, Jennings had served time in prison. He later moved to Lawton and resumed the practice of law. After he received a presidential pardon in 1907, Jennings sought various political offices. Courtesy Carl Albert Center Congressional Archives, University of Oklahoma.

but if such happens he never forgets. Their confidence is not easily or quickly secured, and if they ever have cause to mistrust a white man then such man is off their list forever. Knowing of their history and the treatment accorded them by our government, I was always sympathetic to their efforts to provide educational opportunities for their children to the end that they might better protect themselves in dealing with the white man, and eventually to see their children able to take their place as full citizens of our country. . . .

From the date of my arrival in 1900, the efforts to secure statehood for Oklahoma Territory and Indian Territory constantly increased. Conferences and conventions were held frequently in order to prove to the Congress that the two territories were ready to take their place as a single state in the federal union. However, it was not until June 16, 1906, that the Congress passed the legislation authorizing the convening of a convention to prepare and submit a Constitution joining the two territories in a new state to be known as "Oklahoma."

OKLAHOMA STATE SENATOR, 1907–1920

The constitutional convention was held during the winter of 1906–1907 and the work was completed on July 16, 1907. As provided by resolution, an election was held on September 17, 1907, to accept and approve the Constitution and the vote was overwhelmingly in favor of approval.

Prior to the ratification of the Constitution, the two major political parties agreed to hold a voluntary primary election on June 10, 1907, to select candidates for most of the new offices to be created by the approval of the Constitution. Federal, state, and county officials, save members of the national House of Representatives, were nominated in such primary. The candidates for Congress were selected by district conventions. In such primary election I was nominated to represent the 17th state senatorial district, embracing the counties of Comanche, Stephens, and Jefferson. Along with the approval of the Constitution, I was elected a state senator.

With the Constitution approved by the voters and a full set of federal, state, and county officials elected, we had to await the approval of the Constitution by President Theodore Roosevelt and the fixing of the date for admission of Oklahoma as the 46th state of the

Union. The Constitution was approved and the date of admission
was fixed by the president for November 16, 1907. On such date
the new state government was inaugurated at Guthrie, the then
state capital. An immense crowd, filling to overflowing the capital
city, witnessed the inaugural ceremonies wherein C. N. Haskell was
sworn in as the first governor.[4]

While the voters had selected Robert L. Owen[5] and Thomas P.
Gore[6] to serve as United States senators, yet there was no law authorizing such proceedings, so that the first official act of the new
governor was to sign the credentials appointing the two Democratic
selectees as the two senators to represent the state in the Senate of the United States. The first legislature assembled, as per
call and proclamation of the governor, in Guthrie on December 2,
1907, and remained in session for six months. The long session
proceeded to further organize the new state by the selection of sites
for the necessary normal schools [and] penal and eleemosynary
institutions.

After working almost constantly in the enactment of laws creating the necessary boards and commissions, and making appropriations to cover the salaries and expenses of the new officials, as well
as the appropriations to start construction of the new institutions,
we found at the end of the session that our appropriations for all
purposes totaled almost $3 million. Those who opposed statehood
were violently critical of the vast amount appropriated to launch
the new state government. Many of the legislators shared a conviction that they had appropriated about all the money that they knew
existed. All this meant that the citizens of the new state had not
been educated in the practice of either paying taxes or collecting
revenues.[7]

When statehood came to Oklahoma and Indian Territories, the
Enabling Act designated Guthrie as the temporary capital and provided that no change should be made prior to the year 1913. The
act also provided that the capital should "be located by the electors

of said State at an election to be provided for by the legislature,"
and that no public moneys of the state should be appropriated for
the erection of buildings for capitol purposes prior to 1913.

The inhibition against the people of the new state selecting
their capital for a period of some six years was contested in the
courts, wherein it was held that Congress had no power to bind
the state as to the location of its seat of government. However,
under the restrictions sought to be imposed, the capital remained
at Guthrie until the electors decided the issue in an election held
on June 11, 1910.

The election was held pursuant to an initiated bill designated
as State Question No. 15. The bill provided, among other things,
that the Oklahoma state capital should be removed from Guthrie
and established at Oklahoma City. As an inducement to make the
change, representatives of organizations at Oklahoma City promised the voters that they would provide a free site and, in addition, would raise and donate $1 million for the construction of the
capitol. An additional promise was made to the effect that the city
would provide office space with free rent until a building could be
constructed.

Prior to such election a bond in the sum of $100,000 was pre-
pared and executed to guarantee performance of the promises
made. On such promises and for reasons sufficient to a majority of
the electors, the capital was voted away from Guthrie and established at Oklahoma City.

On the night of election day, when the returns were known and
Oklahoma City had won, the then governor C. N. Haskell procured
the official state seal and motored to Oklahoma City and, with such
seal in his possession, opened up for business at the new capital of
the state on the following morning. When the next session of the
legislature convened at the new capital, we found the governor and
a few of the state officials occupying space in an abandoned ward
school building and other state departments were scattered over

the city in such space as could be procured. There being no one in the new administration with authority to act, the State Senate assumed to take the lead in the matter of securing and approving a site and then to finance the construction costs.

At that particular time a majority of the electors had just voted for Oklahoma City, yet a large number of the citizens of the state were not pleased with the new location. The citizens of Guthrie and the adjacent area were angry because of the loss of the seat of the state government. Other cities had harbored ambitions to become the capital. Then there had been developed sentiment for a plan to go into the countryside, select and procure a large tract of land, construct the capitol in the center, and then locate around the main building such state schools and institutions as had not already been permanently established. This utopian proposal, designated as the "New Jerusalem," had many supporters both in and out of the legislature.

The scarcity of taxable property, the division of interests and sentiment, and [the absence of] . . . precedents made the task of organizing the two territories into one state and the building of a capitol major problems for the legislature. While Oklahoma City had promised free office rent, a free site for the capitol, and $1 million with which to construct the building, we could not locate any person who seemed anxious to make good such promises.

Under the Oklahoma Constitution, in order to obligate the state in a sum in excess of $400,000, the proposal must be submitted to the electors for a vote and thereby approved by a majority of all votes cast for and against the proposal at such election. With conditions existing at that time, no one in authority even suggested that a proposal to issue bonds to defray costs of building the capitol be submitted to the voters for approval. At that time, prior to World War One, the lowest estimate of the cost of a capitol with the then current low prices of materials and wages, ran considerably above $1 million.

As chairman of the State Senate Committee on Appropriations, I was confronted with the problem of financing the construction of the building. The known opposition to a bond issue to finance construction, we were convinced, would be organized to defeat an appropriation; hence, we were forced to realize that nothing could be done at once and that the proposal might be delayed indefinitely. Having been a legislator since statehood, I did not lose hope, as I knew that the problem had to be solved.

My legislative experience had taught me that it was hazardous to try to locate a state institution at some definite point and in the same bill propose an appropriation to construct the project. However, it was not difficult to secure approval of a town for an institution if no costs were attached to the proposal. I remembered that the capitol had been located at Oklahoma City, but not on any definite site, either within or adjacent to such city. I further remembered that there were to be no expenses to the voters and taxpayers because of such change in location.

The building problem confronting us was to secure performance on the promises made by the spokesmen for Oklahoma City. After spending much time and exerting great effort, we were forced to make the threat that unless the promises were made good, the location of the permanent capital would again be submitted to the electors of the state. This strategy was successful, and satisfactory sites for the capitol and governor's mansion, along with 650 acres of land immediately adjacent or nearby, were donated for public uses.

With the land secured, the next step was to get the money for construction of the necessary buildings. Had we known at that time that there was a vast pool of oil under the land secured, our financial problem would have been solved. However, some years after title to the land had been secured and the capitol constructed, oil was discovered on adjacent lands. The state leased the capitol grounds; oil was found and millions of dollars in royalties have been secured for the state treasury; hence, not knowing that the capitol and the governor's mansion were in fact resting on "black gold," and the state being very poor, we had a problem to find the money to build the capitol.

In our search for funds we learned that in territorial days unused appropriations, instead of reverting to the treasury, remained in the original special account and a tabulation of these "odds and ends" accumulated from 1889 to 1907 amounted to $252,224.40. This sum became the "nest egg" of the Capitol Building Fund.

The campaign promise of one million dollars in cash to build the capitol was not made good, so we had to proceed against the persons signing the bond. Not desiring to try to enforce compliance, we agreed to accept the amount of the bond and thereby cancel all claims against the organizations and individuals who were on record as having made the promises. To get the $1 million, the amount of the bond, the electors of Oklahoma City voted a bond issue for park improvement purposes and from the proceeds of each issue the amount of the performance bond was paid into the Capitol Building Fund.

The next item concerned the matter of free rent for office space until the capitol could be made ready for occupancy. At about that time a complaint against the local telephone company was filed with the Corporation Commission, charging that excessive rates were being levied and collected. After a hearing, the commission found that the telephone patrons were entitled to refunds for overpayments. The fact that there were several thousand persons entitled to nominal refunds presented a problem of expense to the telephone company.

A proposal was made and accepted whereby the local citizens' committee would secure from telephone subscribers waivers of refunds due on condition that such refunds would be accepted by the state in lieu of all rents paid and to be paid for office space in the new state capitol. Under this proposal, the sum of $71,200 was secured and the amount was added to the Capitol Building Fund.

The legislature had enacted legislation creating a State Game Commission and provided that persons desiring to hunt should first secure licenses and pay for same the fees prescribed by law. At that time the state had not established either game farms or fish hatcheries, so that a sizeable fund had accumulated. Inasmuch as there was no immediate use for such funds, a bill was introduced and passed authorizing the borrowing of the sum of $94,197.10 from such fund with the provision that such sum borrowed should be repaid from revenues to be secured from the sale of surplus state capitol lands. This money likewise was added to the Capitol Building Fund.

From the sources mentioned, the Capitol Building Fund was built up to the sum of $517,621.50, but such amount was only about one-third of the estimated cost of the capitol. To get the balance of the necessary funds, two additional steps had to be taken. . . .

In order to make some direct contribution toward constructing the capitol, the legislature appropriated the sum of $250,000, which amount was added to the Capitol Building Fund. When such sum was made available, the Capitol Building Fund contained $767,621.50. In order to get actual construction under way, and not having enough money in sight to let a contract, the legislature authorized the State Capitol Commission to approve plans and specifications for the building and then to proceed on a "force account" plan of construction [whereby state agencies provided the labor and equipment].

The record shows that the permanent capital was located at Oklahoma City during the administration of Governor C. N. Haskell and that the actual work of construction was begun during the administration of Governor Lee Cruce.[8] When Oklahoma's third governor, Robert L. Williams,[9] was inaugurated in January 1915, he found the capitol being constructed under a plan wherein the Capitol Commission was buying the material and hiring the labor on a day-to-day basis.

Governor Williams did not approve of the "force account" construction program and recommended that a contract be let to finish the building. In order to secure bidders to complete the job, we had to raise an additional $750,000. This sum was borrowed from the Public Building Fund, under the jurisdiction of the Commissioners of the Land Office. The loan was authorized and directed by Chapter 241 of the Session Laws of 1915, with a proviso that the amount should be repaid to such fund from the sale of the surplus state capitol lands. Thus, from "odds and ends" of territorial appropriations, the forfeiture of a bond, the diversion of telephone refunds, borrowing from the State Game Fund, borrowing from the Public Building Fund, and a relatively small direct appropriation by the legislature, money was secured to build the Oklahoma State Capitol without a bond issue. . . .

One of the first things I learned as a state senator was that one could secure more legislation through amendments to appropriation bills than could be secured in any other way. As I was chairman of the Senate Committee on Appropriations, all House as well as Senate bills proposing appropriations were referred to my committee. When the House bill proposing funds for the maintenance of the Game and Fish Department was considered, I suggested that we amend the bill by adding the sum of $15,000 for each of the years 1916 and 1917, "for purchasing or propagating and distribution of game fish." The bill, as thus amended, was passed by the Senate and the amendment was concurred in by the House. Obviously it did not occur to the House "professional" [quotes added] objectors to the fish hatchery program that in approving the Senate amendment they had, in effect, enacted legislative authority to locate and construct an indefinite number of fish hatcheries in Oklahoma.

To anyone with no experience in legislative work it may not be clear just how the Senate amendment could authorize the location and construction of even one fish hatchery. However, here is how the authority was used: Through conferences with the then governor Robert L. Williams, I knew that he was sympathetic to the

In 1911, when this portrait was made, Elmer Thomas was president pro tempore of the Oklahoma State Senate. First elected to the legislature in 1907, he served through 1920. Copyright 1911, The Oklahoma Publishing Company.

program for the construction and maintenance of fish hatcheries. So when he had approved the bill, I called his attention to the fact that we had the sum of $30,000 appropriated to "propagate and distribute game fish." When I asked the governor how we could "propagate fish" without hatcheries he immediately caught my point and plan. It was obvious that $30,000 would not go very far if lands had to be purchased and contracts let for the construction of the ponds. However, the details had all been worked out. I suggested that we build two hatcheries—one on the east side and one on the west side of the state.

For the west side hatchery, I proposed that I would secure the necessary lands at Medicine Park and that I would undertake to secure free water from Lake Lawtonka, the water supply for the city of Lawton. Then with the land donated and a free water supply secured, I proposed that the governor select a number of "trusty" prisoners from either the Granite or McAlester institutions and assign them the task of building the ponds. The men under prison sentences had to be housed, clothed, and fed, so the bill for labor would be near zero. Also, the expense of guards would be little, if any, greater in camp than in the prison institutions.

In the construction of both of the Oklahoma prisons much equipment such as horses, mules, and dirt-moving machinery had been acquired, so those items did not present a problem; hence, in order to construct the Medicine Park fish hatchery the only cash outlay was for the services of a general superintendent or foreman and the cost of the pipe necessary to convey the water from Lake Lawtonka to the hatchery located below and almost under the dam. When the west side hatchery had been completed, the second or east side hatchery, located in Bryan County, was begun and completed on approximately the same plan used in constructing the Medicine Park institution.

In 1919, the governor of Oklahoma recommended that the legislature submit a proposal to the electors of the state to approve a bond issue of $50 million to finance the construction of a system of hard-surface public highways. While I knew of the great need for roads and had introduced and secured the passage of the first highway law in the state, yet I was not convinced that we knew enough about hard-surface road building to justify the expenditure of so large a sum during one administration; hence, I opposed the submission of the matter at that time. On the final passage of the proposal to submit the issue, I was one of four senators out of the total of forty-four to vote against the bill.

As a counter proposal, I had submitted a bill proposing to raise special revenues for road building on a "pay as you go" plan. The Oklahoma Legislature followed the leadership of Governor James B. A. Robertson[10] and approved the $50 million road bond proposal. Pursuant to the special law an election was called as required by the Constitution to enable the voters to pass judgment on the matter. Having opposed the submission of the proposal in the State Senate, I could not remain silent when the issue was presented to the people of the state. I made as many speeches against the proposal as opportunities permitted and, in addition, proposed to debate the matter with any person who favored the program. A debate was arranged at McAlester, where I met Senator E. P. Hill.[11]

Thereafter a series of debates was arranged for me to meet Senator R. L. Davidson[12] to discuss the proposal at Muskogee, Lawton, Tulsa, and Enid. The meetings were held at Muskogee and Lawton, but for reasons unknown to me, my opponent failed to appear at Tulsa; hence the meeting at Enid was cancelled. In 1919 statewide campaigns had not become "big business"; hence, but little money was expended either in support of or in opposition to the road bond proposal. A mass meeting in opposition to the bonds was held in Oklahoma City, but no statewide organization was perfected to defeat the issue. However, Carl Williams,[13] editor of the *Oklahoma Farmer-Stockman*, a farm publication with wide circulation throughout the state, joined me in publicly opposing the proposal.

I used my hotel room at Oklahoma City as headquarters, and with a contribution of $100 from Mr. Williams we published a leaflet containing questions and answers and mailed the data to our friends for distribution in their several localities. In so far as I know, the speeches, debates, the single mass meeting, and circulation of the leaflet constituted the entire public campaign and effort to defeat the project. Obviously the sponsors of the bonds were over-confident that the program would be approved, but in the special election the proposal was defeated by more than a 100,000 majority.

The defeat was so decisive that no further effort has been made to vote bonds to either build or improve a statewide highway system. In Oklahoma we raise funds to match federal allocations [as provided in the Federal Aid Road Act of 1916] and under such cooperative system, wherein we "pay as we go," our state is keeping pace with our adjacent states in highway construction and development. . . .

ELECTION OF FIRST OKLAHOMA
UNITED STATES SENATORS

At statehood in 1907, Indian Territory was unorganized; hence, it had no laws, other than such federal laws as were applicable to all unorganized areas. Oklahoma Territory was organized with town, city, county, and a form of territorial government with an appointed governor and an elected legislature, all under the authority of the act of Congress approved June 6, 1890. The election to adopt the Constitution was called by the Constitutional Convention but was held under the territorial election laws.

Prior to statehood there was no primary election law, so that candidates for such offices as were elective were nominated in county and district conventions. At that time United States senators were elected by the respective state legislatures; however, the Oklahoma

Constitution provided for a mandatory primary system for the nomination of all candidates for elective offices.

In order to comply with the spirit of the new Constitution, the Democrats of the state met in a mass meeting and entered into a gentlemen's agreement to select nominees for the U.S. Senate in the same primary which was to be held to select state and county nominees. In the gentlemen's agreement it was provided that the state would select one senator from the east side, or from the Indian Territory area, and one from the west side, or from the organized Oklahoma Territory. In such agreement it was stipulated that all candidates for the Senate should run at large and the one residing on the east side securing the largest number of votes over the entire state should be the Democratic nominee from such area, and the candidate residing on the west side who received the largest number of votes from the state at large should be the Democratic nominee from the organized Oklahoma Territory area.

In the primary election the following Democratic candidates filed for the two Senate nominations: Robert L. Owen, residing at Muskogee, on east side; Thomas P. Gore, residing at Lawton, on west side; Roy Hoffman,[14] residing at Chandler, on west side; M. L. Turner,[15] residing at Oklahoma City, on west side; and Henry M. Furman,[16] residing at Ada, on east side. In the primary election, Robert L. Owen received the largest number of votes cast for any candidate; hence, he became the Democratic nominee to represent Oklahoma in the United States Senate from an east side residence. The candidate to secure the second largest number of votes was Henry M. Furman of Ada but, because he resided on the east side of the state, was second to Robert L. Owen, and because of the gentlemen's agreement, he was honor bound to step aside in favor of Thomas P. Gore, a resident of the west side of the state, who had received the largest number of votes from the state at large. While the primary vote was unofficial, yet the Democratic

governor and the Democratic members of the legislature recognized the gentlemen's agreement and the votes cast thereunder
and acted accordingly.

At 12 o'clock noon on November 16, 1907, the two territories became the state of Oklahoma, and the forty-sixth state of the United
States. The first official act of C. N. Haskell, the new governor, was
to appoint and commission Robert L. Owen and Thomas P. Gore to
be Oklahoma's two United States senators. Likewise, one of the first
acts of the first legislature was to elect, officially, the state's two
members of the United States Senate.

After their legal election by the legislature, the two senators drew
lots for the long and the short terms, and by such procedure Senator Gore drew the short term, ending March 4, 1909, and Senator
Owen drew the long term, ending March 4, 1913. In the 1908 primary election Senator Gore was renominated for a second term,
but again he had to be re-elected by the legislature.

The Seventeenth Amendment to the Constitution providing for
the election of United States senators by direct popular vote was not
approved until May 31, 1913; hence, the legislature had to re-elect a
senator in 1909. At high noon on Wednesday, January 20, 1909, the
two houses met in joint session for the purpose of electing a United
States senator. In placing the name of Thomas P. Gore before the
joint session for re-election, I spoke as follows:

"Mr. President, Mr. Speaker, Fellow Representatives: . . . On the
22nd of November, a year ago, *Collier's Weekly,* one of the great
papers of the East, stated, editorially, that Oklahoma was preparing
to send to the United States Senate an Indian and a blind man. . . . It
may be true that the other of those gentlemen has been deprived of
the priceless blessing of sight, it may be true that before his eyes has
been drawn the veil of darkness forever, but if it is, he is a man who
can and will see more in the interests of the people of this state and
nation than could or would the trust-hobbled senators of the East
had they the sight of ten thousand eyes. It is for him I come today to

speak. From Mississippi to Texas, from Texas to Oklahoma, and from Oklahoma to the nation, unaided and alone, without influence or wealth, he has won success until today he stands upon an eminence without a parallel in the history of the world.

"Henceforward and in the future the fight in Congress will be, not between Democrats and Republicans, but a fight between the people and unfair corporations; a fight, not between labor and capital, but a fight between honest labor and dishonest capital; and in this election, here today, unfair corporations and dishonest capital have gained an enemy while the people have won a friend and champion. . . . "

CONGRESSMAN FROM OKLAHOMA, 1923–1927

From statehood in 1907 to 1921, my home city of Lawton was represented in the House of Representatives by Scott Ferris [D-Okla.] and in the United States Senate by Thomas P. Gore. In 1920 our congressman decided to leave the House and try for the Senate — the office held by our fellow townsman, Senator Gore.

When I learned that the position in the House was to become vacant, I resigned from the State Senate and announced my candidacy to succeed Mr. Ferris. The outcome of the 1920 primary election was as follows: Scott Ferris[17] defeated Senator Gore for the Senate and I was nominated for Congress. The result of the general election was not to our liking for the reason that Oklahoma went Republican and both Mr. Ferris and I were defeated. Such defeat brought about a set-back but not undue discouragement as I continued my campaign and was renominated and elected in 1922. In 1924 I was re-elected to Congress without opposition.

In 1920 our state was represented in the Senate by two Republicans — W. B. Pine[18] and John W. Harreld.[19] Senator Harreld had defeated Scott Ferris in 1920; hence, his term was to expire on March 4, 1927. Oklahoma being a Democratic state, I decided to leave the House and try for the Senate. I did not have serious trouble in being elected and remained in the upper branch of the Congress until January 3, 1951. In my twelve campaigns for legislative offices I never once tried to unseat a Democratic incumbent. In legislative work the longer a representative or a senator is retained in office the more efficient and valuable he becomes; hence, conscious of the interests of my constituents, I never thought that I, as a newcomer and a beginner at the bottom of committees that no older member wanted, could secure results comparable to an incumbent with experience and the best committee assignments attained by reason of his seniority.

As in war and football, there is no substitute for victory. Likewise, in legislative work, there is no substitute for experience obtained through seniority or long service. Scott Ferris became a member of the House of Representatives six years before the appearance of Sam Rayburn [D-Tex.][20] the present Speaker; hence, had he chosen to remain in the House he would have had every opportunity of becoming the Speaker, the third highest office within the gift of the people. Had Senator Gore remained in the Senate he certainly would have become chairman of the all-important and powerful Committee on Finance. It is the holders of such top positions who dictate and control the policies of our government.

RED RIVER LANDS

Early in my service in the House of Representatives I introduced a bill "[a]uthorizing payment of all money received as royalty from the Red River oil lands to the Kiowa, Comanche and Apache Tribes of Indians, and for other purposes." The facts upon which the bill was predicated were as follows:

My hometown of Lawton was located almost in the center of what was known as the Kiowa, Comanche, and Apache Indian [lands] ...; hence, the members of the three tribes, to the number of some

3,563, resided adjacent to or near my home in Oklahoma. Origi-
nally the government considered the various Indian tribes as dis-
tinct entities or nations and dealt with such Indians on a treaty basis.

On such a basis the government made a treaty with such tribes
on October 18, 1865, wherein their boundaries . . . were defined.
The Indians claimed a large tract of land located in the southwestern part of what was later to become Oklahoma Territory. Neither the government nor the Indians claimed any land located in
Texas, but the Indians claimed they owned all the land to the Texas
boundary line.

At that time, in 1865 and 1867, it was generally understood that
the boundary line between Texas and the Indian country was the
center of [the] Red River, as such river separated the two geograph-
ical areas. Consequently, when the 1867 treaty was made, the southern boundary of the Indians' [land] . . . was fixed as the center of
[the] Red River. The Indians were advised and, therefore, believed
that their lands extended to the state of Texas.

At a later date about 1915, oil was discovered at Burkburnett,
Texas, located adjacent to the Red River and to the south of the Indian land. The oil pool extended to the south bank and under the
Red River bed. Immediately the United States government claimed
all that part of the oil field located under the river bed. Likewise,
the state of Texas made claim to that part of the field located between the center of such river and the south bank thereof. At the
same time, the state of Oklahoma made similar claims to the oil
lands.

The contest was immediately thrown into the courts and the
Supreme Court of the United States held that the true boundary
between the states of Oklahoma and Texas was not the center of the
Red River, but instead was the south bank of such river. Such decision placed all of the river bed in the state of Oklahoma and di-
vested the state of Texas of any and all claims to the newly discovered oil lands under any part of the river bed. However, such

The U.S. House of Representatives Committee on Public Lands discusses policy in 1924. Elmer Thomas is seated third on the left. As a member, Thomas introduced a bill that gave oil royalties from the bed of the Red River to the Kiowa, Comanche, and Apache Indians. Courtesy Carl Albert Center Congressional Archives, University of Oklahoma.

court decision seemed to give color to the claim of the state of Oklahoma. The contest resulted in the appointment of a receiver for all the property in litigation.[21]

The effect of the decision of the Supreme Court was as follows: The boundary line between the states of Oklahoma and Texas is the south bank of [the] Red River; the land between the center of [the] river and the State of Texas is public domain and located in Oklahoma; the south boundary of the Indians' [land] . . . is the center of [the] river; and all oil discovered and produced on the disputed territory belongs to the United States and the proceeds derived from the sale of such oil should be disposed of as provided by existing law.

Thus, under the decision of the court, the Indians had no legal claim to the oil produced from the center of the river to the south bank thereof, so my problem was to figure out a program to present to the Congress in order to secure for my Indian constituents the royalties from the oil produced from said lands. . . . To me it was obvious that had the government's treaty makers known that the true boundary was the south bank of the river, such boundary line would have been written into the treaty. I contended that the government had made an honest mistake and that in dealing with its wards, the government should not take advantage of the mistake, and therefore, the claim of the Indians that their [land] . . . hence, rights (extended to the state of Texas), should be recognized and admitted.

Based upon such reasoning, I prepared and introduced . . . H.R. 178, Sixty-eighth Congress, First Session, "A BILL Authorizing payment of all money received as royalty from the Red River oil lands to the Kiowa, Comanche, and Apache Tribes of Indians, and for other purposes. . . . " At my request hearings were called to begin on April 30, 1924. Such hearings were held by the House Committee on Public Lands under the direction of the Hon. Nicholas J. Sinnott [R-Ore.], chairman. At the hearings I presented the case for the Indians. . . . My testimony in support of the bill covered some 30 pages of the Congressional Record and was an effort to convince the committee that in order to do justice to the three Indian tribes and give them the benefit of the oil royalties, the southern boundary of their [land] . . . should be considered as having been changed from the center to the southern bank of [the] Red River. . . . The hearings lasted for a number of days and during the proceedings the committee sought to find out just what representations were made to the Indians at the time the 1867 treaty was made. . . . When the hearings were concluded the committee approved the measure and ordered the bill reported to the House calendar. Later the measure was approved and passed by both houses of the Congress and became Public Resolution, No. 36, Sixty-ninth Congress. Under the act, the three tribes of Indians have received to date upwards of $3 million in oil royalties.

IRRIGATION IN OKLAHOMA

I was personally familiar with conditions in the southwestern portion of Oklahoma due to the fact that I represented a farm loan company operating in that section. In addition to personal knowledge of the lack of rainfall, I had firsthand information as to the value of irrigation on a small individual project on Turkey Creek. For a number of years I had been convinced that irrigation would be of great value in producing farm products in western Oklahoma.

As a member of the Oklahoma State Senate I had secured the passage of a comprehensive law providing for the organization and financing of the development of irrigation districts and projects in our state. At the same time, I secured an appropriation to make a test of the benefits of irrigation on a small tract of land connected with the Cameron Agriculture College, located at my hometown of Lawton.

Also, I had been able to have my home city get behind a proposal to use the Lawton mountain water supply to irrigate some 2,500 acres of land located to the northwest and adjacent to the city. Lawton tendered the necessary water. The owners of the land had organized a district; and through the efforts of Congressman Ferris and Senator Gore, both residents of Lawton, the Congress had appropriated the sum of $100,000 to start the project. C. T. Pease, a representative of the Bureau of Reclamation, had been stationed at Lawton to supervise the development. When the work was just being started, World War One came to the United States and as a result Camp Doniphan was located on the Fort Sill Military Reservation. This made it necessary for the city of Lawton to divert its water supply from possible irrigation to military uses, so the proposed project was abandoned.

In 1922 I was elected to Congress, and while I did not lose my interest in irrigation, I was not able to make any substantial progress toward the development of a program until 1936. . . . After a few years in [the Senate], . . . I had been able to be assigned to the Committees on Agriculture and on Appropriations. Being familiar with the facts and in addition having membership on the two all-important committees, I was awaiting the opportunity to renew my efforts to develop an experimental irrigation project in western Oklahoma in order to make a test of the benefits to be derived from the use of water in the production of farm crops. In 1936, the year of our greatest drought, my opportunity came. Because of general drought and the consequent hard times, President Franklin D. Roosevelt called a conference to be held late in the summer at Des Moines, Iowa. Along with other states, Oklahoma sent a delegation to confer with the president at the Iowa capital.

The president conferred with each state delegation separately and when our time came the president inquired as to what plan or plans we had developed to help Oklahoma. In the conference I suggested that western Oklahoma did not have the rainfall that comes to the eastern portion of the state and that to help the west side I proposed that an experimental irrigation project be estab-

lished to determine whether or not such a program would be bene-
ficial in the production of crops. I suggested further that there was a
possible project located at Lugert, near the city of Altus in Jackson
County, which was well known to the Bureau of Reclamation. The
president was sympathetic to the suggestion and asked for more
information, whereupon I outlined the plan in some detail. I proposed that the representatives of the government confer with the
officials of Altus with a view of taking over its water supply—the
Lugert dam and reservoir—and in consideration of granting such
city a permanent water supply to use the Lugert site for multiple
purposes, embracing flood control, reclamation, and domestic water supply.

At the end of our conference President Roosevelt asked me to
assemble data respecting the value and necessity for irrigation in
western Oklahoma and send same to him. Before leaving the Iowa
capital I contacted Senator W. C. Austin at Altus and suggested that
he request Dr. Dover P. Trent of the Oklahoma A. & M. College to
meet us at Oklahoma City at the earliest practical date. The conference was arranged and held, at which time Dr. Trent was assigned the task of assembling the data. Dr. Trent and Senator Austin
prepared a brochure or prospectus, giving pertinent information
and statistical data respecting the need for irrigation in western
Oklahoma.

This activity was the real beginning of the construction of the
Jackson County project. . . . In connection with the consideration of
the Interior Appropriations Bill in 1938 for the fiscal year 1939, I
presented and secured approval of an item in the sum of $200,000
for making investigations of the so-called "Dust Bowl" area, and of
such sum I had earmarked the sum of $25,000 for the proposed
Altus Project in Oklahoma. . . . With the funds thus made available,
the respective investigations were made and reports were submitted
to the Congress. . . . In connection with the development of the

project, I was in a favored position in the Senate in that I was chairman of the subcommittee having charge of funds for the U.S. Army Corps of Engineers and also was a member of the subcommittee having control of appropriations for all irrigation projects. State Senator Austin worked out all problems for the officials of the city of Altus as well as for the landowner members of the irrigation district. Because of the varied interests to be considered, the project made progress slowly. The city of Altus had to be satisfied with respect to a permanent domestic water supply; the landowners had to be satisfied that the annual water charges would not be prohibitive; and both the U.S. Army Corps of Engineers and Bureau of Reclamation officials had to be satisfied that the project could be made a success and eventually paid for.

Still another matter delayed construction — the development of World War Two. Because of such war appropriations, materials and manpower were in slack supply. During the war nothing could be done other than to use WPA labor to quarry rock preliminary to the completion of the enlarged dam. In the construction of the project the city of Altus furnished its Lugert dam and reservoir; the U.S. Army Corps of Engineers had contributed the sum of $1,100,000, and the Bureau of Reclamation furnished the balance of the funds necessary to construct the project. The total cost of the multiple-purpose project has been fixed at $13,206,000.

Where formerly crop failures were common, now the land supplied with water is producing over one bale of cotton per acre, some 35 bushels of wheat, 50 bushels of barley, 60 bushels of oats, 500 bushels of potatoes, and as much as seven tons of alfalfa per acre. The owners of the land in the district are pleased with the project, and the value of irrigation in western Oklahoma has been demonstrated to be a success. So successful had been the project and so active had been W. C. Austin in urging and promoting its construction, that I introduced a bill in the Senate proposing to change the name of the Lugert-Altus irrigation project to the "W. C. Austin Project." The bill was passed and approved on May 16, 1947 (Public Law No. 69)....[22]

GRAND RIVER DAM

It required many years of effort to secure the approval and construction of the Grand River (Pensacola) Dam, located in northeast Oklahoma. In 1928 Congressman E. B. Howard [D-Okla.], of the First Oklahoma District, secured $5,000 to be used by the chief of the U.S. Army Corps of Engineers for surveying the Grand River area, along with other flood control projects on the Mississippi River and its tributaries. The survey disclosed that it would cost some $6,263,000 to construct a flood control dam and reservoir at the Pensacola site.

In 1935 the Oklahoma Legislature created the Grand River Dam Authority. Pursuant to the act a board was appointed and efforts were made to finance construction of the project. However, the state authority was unable to finance the project for controlling floods, and with a limited water supply, the authority was unable to secure finances to build a hydroelectric project. This meant that the project would have to be financed by the government for the control of floods on the Grand River.

At that time, only a preliminary survey had been made, so that before the project could be approved for construction a final and complete survey must be made. On May 21, 1936, I offered an amendment to the pending flood control bill in the Senate, proposing to authorize and direct that final surveys be made of the following projects: Eufaula, Pensacola (Grand River), Markham Ferry, Fort Gibson, Wister, Oologah, Mannford, Tulsa–Sand Springs Levee, and Tenkiller Ferry. The amendment was agreed to and the surveys were ordered made.

The Oklahoma delegation made a special effort to secure an

early survey and approval of the Pensacola project. An appeal was
made to President Roosevelt to allocate funds from relief appropriations. . . . The president made funds available and the survey was
completed. The plans were expanded to embrace flood control,
hydroelectric development, and recreation. The estimated cost, because of the enlarged project, was increased to some $20 million.
With project approved, the next task was to get the money to cover
the cost of construction.

On June 21, 1937, during the consideration of the "Public Works
Administration Extension Act," I offered an amendment as follows:
"On page 19, line 20, after the numerals 1937, insert 'for projects
for which revenue bonds have been authorized by State Legislatures under the law of the State where the project is located.'"
Persons not familiar with legislative procedures would hardly understand what such an amendment could possibly mean. While
no project was mentioned specifically, yet the amendment was intended to authorize an appropriation for the construction of the
Grand River Dam and Reservoir. The bill under consideration proposed to authorize appropriations to be used on a cooperative basis
with cities, counties, and states to construct public works in order to
give employment to labor. . . .

Once having secured the authority to appropriate, I offered a second amendment to provide the funds to construct the works. . . . The
two amendments—one to authorize appropriations to construct
projects where a state legislature had created authorities to issue
bonds to finance contributions to such projects; and [the other] to
appropriate the money to pay the government's part of any such
cooperative projects—were agreed to in the Senate, and in conference with the House the two amendments were consolidated.

With the legislation completed, the balance of the task was administrative. Under the law the Grand River Dam Authority issued
its bonds and sold same to the government to finance its contribution to the cost of the projects. With the state's contribution,

the government made a grant to the authority of a sum sufficient to build the flood control, hydroelectric, and recreational project known as the Grand River Dam and Reservoir.[23]

FLOOD CONTROL THROUGH DAMS AND RESERVOIRS IS AN OKLAHOMA PLAN

Oklahoma, since statehood in 1907, has been intensely interested in the flood control problem. The fact that the state is bounded on the south by the Red River and is crossed by and contains such rivers and streams as the Grand, Illinois, Verdigris, Arkansas, Cimarron, North Canadian, Deep Fork, Little River, South Canadian, Washita, North Fork, Clear Boggy, Muddy Boggy, and Kiamichi caused our citizens to become vitally interested in finding a plan to control the too frequent floods coming to our state.

The Oklahoma Legislature created a special Commission on Drainage, Irrigation and Flood Control to try to work out a plan for the control of floods. The commission employed engineers who made a survey of the rivers and streams of the state. A number of dam and reservoir sites were located and levees were recommended in places. The program developed came to be known as the "Blake Plan" for the control of floods.

The hearings held in 1928 were with respect to whether the dike-levee system should be continued and expanded, or a program embracing dams and reservoirs should be adopted and developed. The Blake Plan called for the construction of dams and reservoirs on the upper reaches of the streams and rivers for the purpose of catching and holding the water where it falls, thus keeping such water from flowing into the streams and rivers so swiftly and in such quantities as to cause disastrous floods.

At the time of the 1928 hearings the Corps of Engineers favored a continuation of the dike and levee system to control floods. To show what great changes have taken place, the House committee had before it a report from the Chief of Engineers in which, among other things, it was stated: "It is axiomatic that States and other local authorities should supply all the land and assume all pecuniary responsibilities for damages that may result from the execution of the project. . . . It would be revolutionary for the Federal Government to establish the precedent of buying part of the land upon which to build protective works to increase the value of the remainder. . . ."

In 1933 the Congress passed the Tennessee Valley Authority Act in which it was provided that the government should bear all costs connected with land acquisition, dam construction, operation, and maintenance. The T.V.A. Act was the precedent which changed the program for flood control. It was well known by the engineers that electric energy could not be produced economically from dams and reservoirs in the Tennessee Valley area if all the costs were to be charged against the power created; hence, to formulate a plan for the consideration of the Congress and the country, it was provided that the public moneys to be expended should be "in the interest of the national defense and for agricultural and industrial development, and to improve navigation in the Tennessee River and Mississippi River Basins."

With the T.V.A. Act for a guide, Major General E. M. Markham, Chief of Engineers, in his report to the Secretary of War on April 6, 1937, recommended the construction of a large number of flood control reservoirs on the tributaries of the Ohio and Mississippi Rivers with all costs of land, construction, and operation to be borne by the United States. At the time, Phil Ferguson [D-Okla.], representing the Eighth Oklahoma Congressional District, was a member of the House Committee on Flood Control. Through his position on the House authorizing committee and through my position on the Senate Committee on Appropriations, we, with the cooperation and support of the entire Oklahoma delegation, working together, had no difficulty in securing approval of projects in our state. . . .

SALE OF CHOCTAW-CHICKASAW
COAL-ASPHALT DEPOSITS

On June 28, 1898, the U.S. government approved a treaty made
with the Choctaw-Chickasaw Nations and known as the Atoka
Agreement, wherein the members of the two Indian nations agreed
to accept individual allotments; to surrender their tribal forms of
government after an eight-year period deemed necessary to terminate such governments; and to become, in effect, wards of the
United States. However, in such treaty it was provided that at the
end of such eight-year period the members of the two tribes should
"become possessed of all the rights and privileges of citizens of the
United States." In such treaty, all coal, asphalt, and other mineral
deposits were reserved to the said nations. But such deposits were to
be managed, leased, and disposed of under rules and regulations to
be made by the Secretary of the Interior. In the making of the said
treaty the Indians were led to believe that a sale of the reserved coal
and mineral deposits would be arranged by the government. In a
short period of time they were to cease to exist as nations and were
to become full citizens of the United States. When that time should
arrive the members hoped to be able to end and liquidate their
tribal affairs and property.

Later, on July 1, 1902, the Congress enacted legislation wherein
the agreement made by the Commission of the Five Civilized
Tribes . . . was ratified and confirmed. The said mentioned agreement, "ratified and confirmed" by the Congress, contained a provision requiring the government to sell "at public auction for cash
under the direction of the President, the deposits of coal and
asphalt."

When statehood came in 1907 nothing had been done about the
sale of the said mineral deposits. The Indians wanted to sell the
deposits so that a final settlement could be had with the government. Bills were introduced in the Congress but no action was taken

Congressman Wilburn Cartwright (D-Okla.) and Senator Elmer Thomas examine papers concerning Indian affairs. Congressman Will Rogers (D-Okla.) stands behind them. Because of the large Indian population in Oklahoma, it was not surprising that all three men served on the Indian Affairs committees. As the chairmen of their respective committees, Senator Thomas and Congressman Rogers authored the Oklahoma Indian Welfare Act of 1936. Courtesy Carl Albert Center Congressional Archives, University of Oklahoma.

on such measures. Later, oil and gas were discovered in Oklahoma and the value of the coal deposits was thereby depreciated. However, the Indians continued their efforts to dispose of their once valuable coal lands. Even with gas and oil competition, there was a demand for coal, so that some of the mines continued to be operated.

The vast properties were under the supervision of the Interior Department; hence, it required a number of persons to look after the making of leases, supervise mining operations, and collect the rentals and royalties. The records disclosed that the income from the mining and sale of the minerals was being consumed by the salaries and expenses of the managers of the properties. This meant that in time the deposits would be depleted and that the members of the two tribes would never realize anything from their jointly held coal and asphalt deposits.

During the half century that the Indians had been forced to keep the deposits due to the fact that they were without authority to negotiate a sale themselves, it had been impossible to secure favorable action on bills proposing a sale direct to either private interests or to the government. Such bills, providing for the sale of coal deposits, are considered private legislation due to the fact that only a relatively few individuals are interested and affected. In the Congress all such bills when approved by a committee are placed on the unanimous calendar, where a single objection defeats favorable action.

During all the years, relief for the Indian seemed hopeless. Congressmen Charles Carter, William W. Hastings, Wilburn Cartwright, and Thomas D. McKeown had tried to find a way to help the members of the Choctaw and Chickasaw tribes. During the time mentioned, I had been chairman and was still a member of the Senate Committee on Indian Affairs and, in addition, had a high place on the Appropriations Committee.

In 1944, when the bill proposing funds to support the Bureau of

Indian Affairs came to the Senate, I had a plan ready to submit to the committee respecting the sale of the mineral deposits of the two tribes of Indians. In the Senate the rules do not permit . . . adding legislation to appropriations bills, and it required legislation to either authorize or permit anything to be done about the sale of the coal and asphalt lands. Under the procedure in the Senate, a committee chairman or a high-ranking member of a committee has every opportunity of securing favorable action on any proposal containing merit. To me, the sale of the mineral-bearing lands was not only advisable but absolutely necessary if the Indians were ever to get anything for their interests therein. All along, the revenue derived from leases and royalties was being used for expenses of supervising and managing the lands.

In considering a plan of procedure, I decided to ask the Appropriations Committee to assist in closing the affairs of the Choctaw-Chickasaw tribes of Indians by accepting an amendment to the Interior appropriations bill, then pending before such committee. The amendment had been carefully prepared in conferences with Floyd Maytubby, governor of the Chickasaw Nation; Earl Welch, a Chickasaw Indian, and member of the Oklahoma State Supreme Court; and Ben Dwight, a former chief of the Choctaw Tribe. . . . The committee recognized the merits of the proposal and added the amendment to the bill carrying funds to support the Interior Department for the 1945 fiscal year. The fact that the text recited that it was the fulfillment of the Atoka Agreement with the Choctaw-Chickasaw Nations of Indians caused the amendment to be accepted by both the Senate and House with scarcely a question being asked.

The further fact that a number of separate steps were provided as safeguards to both the Indians and the government answered the criticisms of those who were not acquainted with the history of the efforts to sell the properties. All the steps proposed were taken in order and now, after some 50 years of constant effort, the members

of the two nations are receiving their per capita payments from the
approximately $8,500,000 appropriated by the Congress. . . .[24]

FORTY-HOUR WEEK

In 1934 the Great Depression was still being felt in the United
States. While prices had improved and times were growing better,
yet the number of unemployed was very great. All friends of wage
earners were seeking programs for their relief. At that time men
employed in the Navy Yards and in government shops and plants
were working six days per week and sometimes more than eight
hours per day. The suggestion was made that if such wage earners
were limited to a five-day week and an eight-hour day, then the
government could divide up its necessary work and thereby employ
a larger number of persons. As a program to give a larger number of
wage earners jobs, the suggestion appealed to me as being sound.

At that time, the bill proposing to make "appropriations for
the Executive Office and sundry independent executive bureaus,
boards, commissions, and offices, for the fiscal year ending June 30,
1935," was being considered on the Senate floor. In conferences
with Mr. N. P. Alifas, president and district representative of District Lodge 44, National Association of Machinists, an amendment
to the pending bill was . . . introduced. . . . The amendment, as
passed by the Senate, was accepted without change by the House
and thereby became Section 23 of the bill that was sent to the
president for his approval. For reasons stated in his message, but
not because of the 40-hour per week amendment, President Roosevelt vetoed the bill. On March 27, 1934, the House of Representatives passed the bill notwithstanding the veto of the president, and
on March 28, 1934, the Senate took similar action on the measure
and thereby said bill containing the amendment became a law.

On August 26, 1949, during the discussion of a motion made by
me . . . I had the following to say about the 40-hour week amend-

ment which became a law in 1934, some 15 years before: ". . . That little provision of law, adopted to the 1934 bill, has become the cornerstone of the entire working movement in the United States, although at that time it was intended, as I thought, to apply only to the Navy. Later it was applied to the entire Naval Establishment, and later the principle has been made applicable to all Federal employees, even those in the Civil Service. Not only that but even the private industries are now working under the 40-hour week, and only recently the railroad brotherhoods made contracts with the railroads of the United States, and the 40-hour week is the basis of those contracts. . . ."

PUBLIC ROADS ACROSS INDIAN RESERVATIONS IN MINNESOTA AND OKLAHOMA

For many years the state of Minnesota had plans perfected for the construction of a public highway to be located near and along the west coast of Lake Superior, from the city of Duluth on the south to a connection with an improved Canadian highway at the Canadian border and to be known as State Trunk Highway 61, also designated as United States Highway Number 61. . . . At the identical time that the state of Minnesota was being denied the opportunity to build a highway across an Indian reservation, my state of Oklahoma had a like application pending to build a highway across the Seneca Indian School property, located in Ottawa County, which application was later likewise rejected.

At that time I was chairman of the Senate Committee on Indian Affairs and was familiar with the procedure respecting Indian legislation. When a bill relating to Indians was introduced in the Senate, it was referred to my committee for consideration. The first step in such consideration was to send a copy of the bill to the Secretary of the Interior with a request that the committee be advised of his reaction and recommendations with respect to said measure.

In 1936 Thomas (sixth from the left) poses with American Indians and others at Glacier Park Station, Montana. Courtesy Carl Albert Center Congressional Archives, University of Oklahoma.

In instances where the secretary was favorable to such bill, he would report by an official letter, and when he opposed favorable action, he would likewise report his opposition. In most cases the committee would concur in the recommendations made by the secretary, and only in rare cases did the committee recommend bills favorably when the Interior Department opposed the measure. There were . . . compelling reasons for such committee actions: First, if the committee reported a bill for passage with an adverse departmental recommendation, then such bill invited objections when it came up for consideration on the Senate calendar; and if the bill, with an adverse report, was passed by the Senate, the adverse report followed the bill to the House, and as a rule, that was the last ever heard of the legislation. However, if the bill was also passed by the House, it had to be approved by the president before it became a law.

The presidential procedure on legislation is as follows: When a bill is passed by the Congress it is messaged to the president, and immediately upon reaching the White House the bill is referred to the department having jurisdiction of the subject matter. If the bill is opposed by the department, then the reasons for such opposition are set forth in a letter or memorandum to the president. Bills affecting only a few persons are referred to as private measures, and when the department opposes the enactment of such proposals, the president, as a rule, returns such bills to the Congress with veto messages. It is a rare occasion when the Congress passes a private bill over the veto of the president. . . .

Knowing of the . . . opposition of the Interior Department to the Minnesota and Oklahoma road proposals, we did not choose to waste time and effort in a practically hopeless task. . . . With respect to the requests of the two states for permission to construct highways across Indian [lands] . . . , there was no way to gain the authority save through legislation and no way to secure the necessary legislation save through a rider on the Interior Department ap-

propriations bill. Consequently, I prepared the amendments and
offered same during the committee consideration of the Interior
bill. The only arguments necessary to secure favorable action by
the committee were the recommendations of the two states acting
through their respective highway departments.

When a senator has served long enough to secure membership
on the Appropriations Committee, he knows that there is no other
way to secure favorable action on such private bills save through
amendments to an appropriation bill. When a legislative rider is
once attached to an important appropriations bill, it is safe as the
president does not often veto such measures.

In the two instances referred to — one for Minnesota and the
other for Oklahoma — I offered the amendments in the committee
and same were agreed to, which meant that I was authorized to offer
the amendments on the Senate floor with no objections from the
members of the committee. As the items were matters local to the
two states, no objections were made on the floor, so the amendments became a part of the appropriations bill. The only remain-
ing obstacle was to get by the conference committee, which in the
instances mentioned was not difficult. The two amendments became a part of the bill which was approved by the president on
July 2, 1942. . . .

BONUS FOR VETERANS

Shortly after the end of World War One, an effort was initiated to
secure from the government an adjustment with respect to the pay
received by the men in uniform during such war. . . . At that time the
administration, being Republican in all branches, did not look with
favor on the proposal. Likewise, many leading Democrats refused to
assist the veterans in their efforts to secure an adjustment in the
form of a bonus or a retroactive allowance on a per diem basis
covering the time of their service in uniform.

During the Congress following the end of the war, bonus bills were introduced in the House and Senate but sufficient support could not be mustered to even secure hearings. In those days the veterans did not have a special committee created to hear their claims and appeals; hence, their bills were referred to the Ways and Means Committee of the House and to the Finance Committee of the Senate.

The veterans had a long and rough road to travel, but as time passed they increased their efforts. Their first success came on May 19, 1924, when they prevailed upon the Congress to enact legislation granting the Adjusted Service Certificates. That first step was necessary in order to make up the rolls of eligible veterans with the amounts due each based upon their record of service.

When the depression came in 1929, many veterans were thrown out of employment and others in business were forced to either liquidate or fail. This meant a demand for the opportunity to cash such adjusted certificates. The demand for the payment of the certificates, denominated "soldiers' bonus," grew until a majority of the House was pledged to enact such legislation.

In the early summer of 1932 business was at a standstill; thousands of veterans were unemployed and economic conditions were gradually getting worse; hence, it was an opportune time for "a move on Washington" to try to influence Congress to provide relief in the form of cash for the adjusted certificates held by the veterans. . . . Upon arrival at the capital the men "camped out" wherever night caught up with them. The city authorities were cooperative and tolerant as they knew that every veteran had at least one congressman and two senators to whom he could appeal in the event of embarrassment or trouble.

Camp sites were set aside for the use of the former soldiers and sailors. However, the men had to provide their own housing, which in a short time embraced shelter of almost every conceivable kind —from tents, shacks made of tin cans and boxes, to abandoned

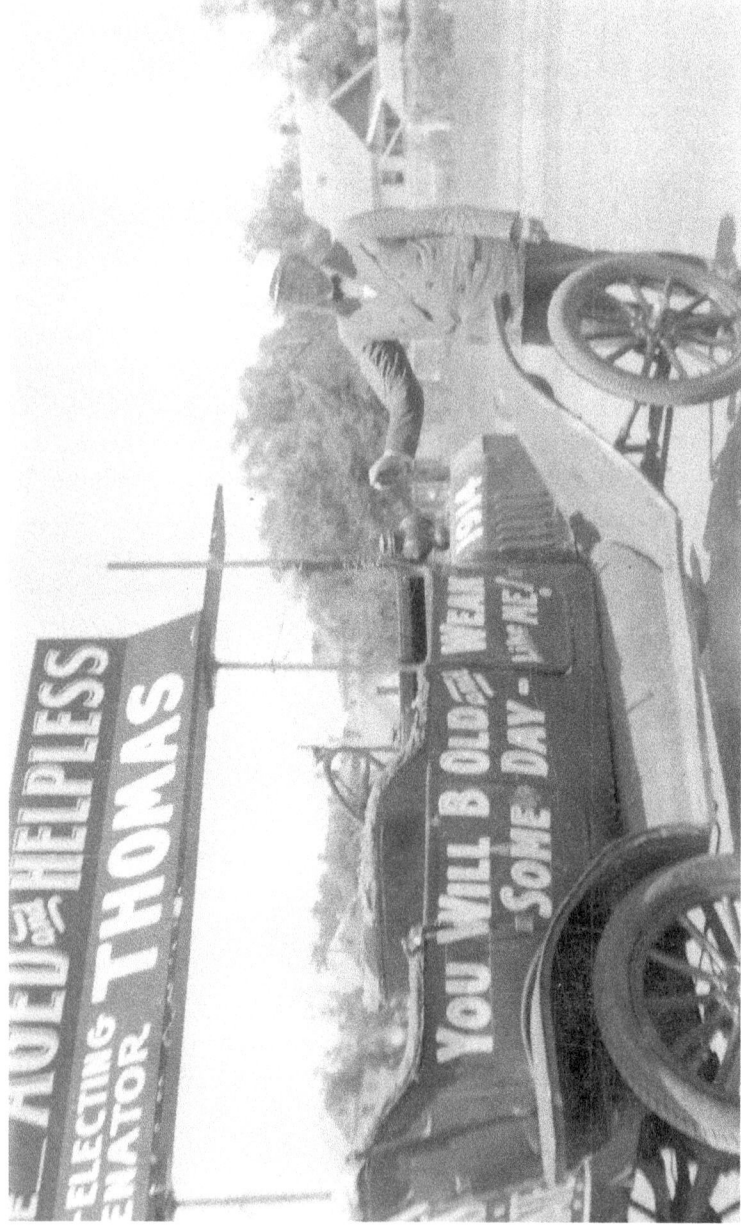

In the throes of the Great Depression, Elmer Thomas spent little money on his campaign in 1932. Focusing on the inadequacies of the Republicans' program to ease the plight of working people, Thomas easily won reelection. Courtesy Carl Albert Center Congressional Archives, University of Oklahoma.

automobile bodies. A very few vacant store and warehouse buildings were used by the veterans. The disabled veterans, drawing compensation, were able to provide and occupy the better accommoda-
tions. The others had to exist the best way they could.

Very soon the "bonus marchers" organized and established a
newspaper for keeping the men advised of their program and
of developments. The veterans, without funds, were able to find
some employment through the sale of the issues of their paper, and
such other articles, including apples, as were permitted by the city
government. In so far as is known, no registration or census was
taken, so the number of veterans in Washington was estimated from
20,000 to 25,000. The largest camp was located on the Anacostia
River and opposite the Navy Yard. The second camp in size was
located near Pennsylvania Avenue and not far from the center of
the city. The men, while desperately in need of assistance, had not
forgotten the discipline they had received and observed during
their active war days. The clothing of the men consisted of whatever
they had, ranging from worn and faded uniforms to sweaters and
overalls. The men selected an official spokesman in the person of
Commander Walter W. Waters, but for the want of funds with which
to operate the "General of the Bonus Marchers" had many occa-
sions to give advice but a few opportunities of giving orders.[25]

Congressman Wright Patman [D-Tex.] . . . , the leader of the
House forces, had the so-called bonus payment bill pending in the
Ways and Means Committee, where it was thought to be securely
"bottled up." However, Congressman Patman was able to secure a
public hearing on his bill, when many witnesses appeared and testified in support of the measure. Along with others, I was invited to
appear before the House Ways and Means Committee on April 12,
1932, when I made the best argument I could in support of the
Patman bill. My testimony, with the questions asked, covered some
30 pages of the House hearings.[26]

The majority of the committee being opposed to the Patman bill

made it necessary to prepare and file a discharge petition in order
to give the veterans a chance to secure relief. By the middle of June
1932, the petition contained sufficient signatures to cause the bill to
be ordered to the House floor for a vote.

In celebration of this success, the veterans staged an historic
parade — not on Pennsylvania but instead on Constitution Avenue,
leading from the Potomac River to the Capitol. Such a parade had
not before been seen in historic Washington. The population of
the capital city is made up in the main of citizens from the states;
hence, all of Washington save the official ruling class and the "cave
dwellers" were sympathetic with the veterans and their program.
The hour of the parade was early twilight and the avenue was lined
with masses of people. No bands were there to lead the thousands
of marchers. The veterans were organized only by states. Crudely
lettered signs separated and designated the motley groups. Such
flags as could be secured were proudly displayed. To accommodate
the disabled who could not walk, a few flat bed trucks had been
donated. . . .

Such [a] parade — it was a victory parade celebrating their success in forcing the bonus payment bill out of the House Ways and
Means Committee where they thought it would soon be voted into
law. With respect to prompt action, the veterans were not disap-
pointed. Immediately the House leaders called up and passed the
bill by a vote of 211 to 176. As promptly as the House acted, President Herbert Hoover announced that he would veto the bill if it
passed the Senate. According to the rules, immediately after the
House action the bill was messaged to the Senate. The Senate leadership, in order to accommodate the veterans and get them out of
Washington, gave the bill special and preferred treatment. The bill
was referred to the Finance Committee and without hearings the
committee, by a vote of 12 to 2, reported the bill back to the Senate
with the recommendation "that it do not pass."

When the bill with a "do not pass" report reached the Senate calendar, it was immediately called up for a vote on final passage. The opposition, with the promised threat of a presidential veto and with an obvious majority of votes against the measure, did not dignify the bill by even explaining the reasons for their opposition.

Because of the meager support in the Senate, . . . the debate did not linger, and in order to give the Patman bill the "coup de grace" the session on June 17, 1932, was extended far into the night. As a former member of the House I had supported the measure . . . and because of the severity of the depression I was supporting the bill in order that the veterans might have such monetary relief as the measure provided. When the House acted favorably on the so-called "bonus bill" the veterans had hopes that the Senate would cooperate in advancing the date from 1945 to 1932 for the payment of the certificate pledges already made.

On the day fixed for the vote in the Senate, for the want of something more impressive to do, the veterans assembled on the Capitol Plaza immediately in front of and adjacent to the Senate wing of the Capitol. As many as could be accommodated were admitted to the Senate galleries, while others were in line for any seat that might be vacated. At no time or place was there any sign of disorder, yet the air was charged with an intense hope that the opposing senators would relent and permit the bill to pass.

Although I was serving my first term in the Senate, I knew in advance that the bill would fail to pass. Nevertheless, I used such time as I deemed proper to make the record and to state my reasons for supporting the measure. While I was addressing the Senate, a page brought to my desk a note advising that a committee representing the assembled veterans was waiting in the office of the Sergeant at Arms to invite me to speak from the steps leading up to the Senate chamber.

Knowing that my Senate speech was falling on deaf ears and fearing that the vast mass of veterans and their friends on the outside might misinterpret an adverse vote on their bill, I closed my floor speech, met the committee, and proceeded to the steps where other speeches had been made. Having worked with the leaders and having visited the several camps, I was recognized when I appeared on the Senate steps, where I addressed the vast throng as follows:

"Veterans, my friends, and I hope you believe that I am your friend. I have just left the Senate floor, where I spoke in your behalf. . . . I have just advised the Senators that your bill is before them backed by a solemn petition signed by more than two and half million veterans.

"The Senators admit that the money is due you. They are convinced that you need the money and the thousands here tonight is convincing proof that you want the money that your government has already admitted that is due you.

"I have just reminded the Senators that already they have granted relief to the larger income taxpayers who are neither ragged nor hungry tonight. I have reminded them that in haste and with enthusiasm they passed a bill making available vast sums of money to be loaned to railroads, insurance companies, and the great corporations of America.

"The United States Senate, representing this administration, has already appropriated billions for big business but not a sou for veterans. Relief has been provided for those who remained at home but nothing has been done to assist you soldiers and sailors who have fought our country's battles. . . ."

After concluding my brief address, I returned to the Senate chamber and after a speech by Senator John H. Bankhead [D-Ala.] . . . , the vote on final passage was recorded. On the roll call of senators the vote was 20 for and 60 against the bill; however, before the vote was officially announced, as per my former statement in the Senate, I changed my vote from "Aye" to "Nay" in order to be qualified to lodge a motion for reconsideration of the vote by which the bill failed of passage. Senator Bankhead likewise changed his vote from "Aye" to "Nay" for the same reason.

When the vote was announced by the vice president, Senator Bankhead and I, simultaneously, addressed the presiding officer, and Senator Bankhead was recognized. The senator proceeded to give the reasons for his vote preliminary to lodging a motion to reconsider. To lodge or enter a motion to reconsider means that a senator, having voted with the majority, may enter on the record a motion to reconsider and then at some later date such senator may call up the motion for consideration and action.[27]

The general practice in the Senate is that when such a motion is entered immediately after a final roll call vote, the bill is held in "status quo" pending action on such motion. Our parliamentary move was to try to hold the bill alive in the hope that we could later muster votes to reconsider the adverse vote and then join the House in passing the bill.

The enemies of the bill had anticipated our strategy, so while Senator Bankhead had the floor Senator Reed Smoot [R-Utah][28] made a point of order that there was no motion before the Senate; hence, there was nothing to talk about and the senator was out of order. The vice president sustained the point of order and Senator Bankhead had to take his seat. . . .

After the bonus bill had been defeated, I secured the floor and made a statement as follows: "Mr. President and Senators, the Chief Executive has vetoed this bill in advance; then, with a vote of 62 to 18 against the veterans, the administration forces, flushed with victory and mad with power, proceeded to give the hopes of the heroes of other days the coup de grace. . . . During those selfsame moments when the Presiding Officer was making new precedents with his unfamiliar rulings, just outside the Senate Chamber and massed across the Capitol Plaza some 20,000 ragged and hungry veterans — some with congressional medals of honor, some with distinguished-service crosses, and many with foreign decorations, but all with heavy hearts and uncovered heads — were singing: 'My country, 'tis of thee, Sweet land of liberty.' History will contrast, appraise, and affix the relative merits of the respective acts of the Senate and the veterans on this historic night." My prophecy made before the veterans in my brief speech on the Capitol steps, that it might require a new Congress and a new administration to pay them the obligations due, came true, and the next Congress, under a different administration, passed a bill providing for the cashing of their Adjusted Service Certificates.

EFFORT TO HELP OIL WORKERS

At one time . . . Oklahoma was the greatest producer of oil and gas in the nation; hence, in order to help the owners of the lands producing such minerals, as well as those engaged in the industry, I favored a fair price for oil products. Fair prices help the farmer-owners of the lands and those who produce the commodities. They also help those who work in the oil and gas fields and those who serve the industry. . . . The treasuries of the districts, counties, and states, including the federal government, [also benefit] through the vast amount of ad valorem, gross production, sales, and income taxes collected and paid out for the support of the various units of government.

In 1929 the Great Depression struck and brought hard times to all and the bankruptcy of a vast number of American industries. The oil industry did not escape the depression and as a result oil sold in Oklahoma and Texas for as low as a few cents per barrel. . . . Many American oil companies had concessions abroad and, being able to employ labor at lower wages than in the states, began flooding America with cheap foreign oil. Such a development reacted adversely to the interests of the small, independent and local oil producers, as well as to the interests of labor employed by the larger, as well as the smaller, companies.

In 1929 the Congress spent most of its time in holding hearings and considering a general tariff measure known as the Hawley-

Smoot Tariff Bill. Being a minority member of the Finance Committee, I attended the hearings and sought to participate in the
development of the new tariff schedules. [As I] represent[ed] a
leading oil-producing state, it was to be expected that I would
have many communications respecting items to be affected by tariff rates.[29]

Some of the oil companies in Oklahoma were subsidiaries of
larger companies, at the time engaged in producing oil in foreign
countries and importing such oil into the United States free of
either tariff or excise taxes. Early during the consideration of the
new tariff measure some of the smaller independent companies
which depended upon the sale of crude oil produced from their
properties complained about the low prices they were receiving and
placed the blame on the larger companies for importing foreign
and cheaper oil in competition with their more costly and expensive product.

As Oklahoma's representative on the Finance Committee, I was
requested to try to secure a tariff of $1.00 per barrel on imported
oil. In view of the fact that my state had such a vast and widespread
interest in oil production, I readily agreed to make the effort.

My first step was to have the committee hold hearings on the
proposal to impose a tariff on oil. I soon realized that I was in for
an all out fight. Due to my inexperience I was under many illu-
sions. The Republican Party controlled the administration in all its
branches. . . . The pending tariff measure took its name from the
chairmen of the respective committees—Congressman Willis C.
Hawley [R-Ore.], chairman of the House Ways and Means Committee, and Senator Reed Smoot [R-Utah], chairman of the Senate
Committee on Finance. Under the Constitution, the House acted
first so that the bill before the Senate committee had already received favorable action in the other branch of the Congress.

In order to develop and record the facts, I requested Chairman
Smoot to appoint a subcommittee to hear the proponents of the oil

tariff amendment I had introduced and had pending before the committee. At that point my fight began, as I discovered that the chairman, although a high tariff Republican, was against a tariff on imported oil. At all times I was treated courteously, but no subcommittee was being named to hear my independent oil-producing friends.

W. B. Pine, my Republican colleague at the time and a substantial producer of oil in Oklahoma, cooperated fully in at first requesting and later demanding that the hearing be granted. I was serving my first term and fully realized my limitations as a member of the all powerful Senate Finance Committee. When it became known that I was supporting a tariff on oil, I was advised that I could get cooperation from the coal industry [and its spokesman, Senator] Harry B. Hawes [D-Mo.]. . . . The fact that oil was in competition with coal as fuel caused the coal people to be willing to join in the effort to restrict their competition.

With the help of my colleagues — Senator Pine and ex-Congressman E. B. Howard [D-Okla.] from the Tulsa oil capital district and Senator Hawes, along with the coal influence — I was able to get the chairman to promise to appoint the necessary subcommittee to hold the hearings. . . . After securing the promise the next thing was to get him to act. Later I learned that Chairman Smoot needed time to make sure that the committee appointed would perform the task in a manner satisfactory to the administration, which was opposed to a tariff in any amount or form being imposed on oil imports.

A new senator has many things to learn and nothing save experience makes lasting and convincing impressions. With the obstacles thrown across my path, I should have realized that a first-term senator at the bottom of the minority side of the committee could hardly expect to win a tariff fight or any kind of a fight against the opposition of the majority party. . . . When Chairman Smoot finally appointed the subcommittee to hear the oil tariff witnesses, it should have been as plain as "hand writing on a wall" that any hearing held would be a farce.

To serve on the subcommittee he appointed the following: Senator David A. Reed [R-Pa.] . . . , reputed to be attorney for one of the larger oil-importing companies; Senator Walter E. Edge [R-N.J.] [30] . . . , reputed to be a brother-in-law of the then head of the Standard Oil Company of New Jersey; and Senator William H. King of Utah, the only "Free Trade" Democrat in the Senate. However, a date for hearing the witnesses favoring a tariff on oil was set and the following persons appeared and testified: Senator Pine of Oklahoma; ex-Congressman E. B. Howard of the Tulsa district; Senator Harry B. Hawes, representing the coal industry; and Harold B. Fell,[31] a prominent independent oil producer from Ardmore, Oklahoma.

In so far as the record shows, the subcommittee never made a report to the full Committee on Finance. In making up the bill preliminary to reporting same to the Senate calendar, I was unable to secure approval of my oil tariff amendment. In the development of the Hawley-Smoot Tariff Bill, it required almost one year to hold hearings and to get the measure through the House. Then it required another six months to get the bill through the Senate.

When debate on the many items covered by the bill began on the Senate floor, I re-offered my oil tariff amendment. During the early months of 1930, times had become increasingly worse; prices had fallen, unemployment had increased, and the depression had reached every segment of our people. Because of existing economic conditions, the demand for an oil tariff likewise increased. Representatives of the independent producers, in an effort to secure favorable action at the hands of the Senate, organized a group of interested oil operators and managers to the number of some 125 and journeyed to Washington in an effort to secure relief from the flood of cheap foreign oil then being imported into the United States.

Oklahoma, being a new state, was made up of citizens from practically all the other states; hence, the oil delegation contained substantial former citizens from almost every state in the nation. Upon
arrival at the capital the delegates organized and proceeded to
contact as many senators as possible in order to explain the plight in
which the oil industry found itself. Headquarters were established at
one of the larger hotels with Wirt Franklin[32] of Oklahoma City in
charge, and the serious business of the special mission was initiated.

In as much as the tariff bill was being considered in the Senate, it
was then too late to secure an additional hearing. The delegation —
at the time designated as the "oil lobby" — had to restrict its work to
personal conferences with senators and to reporting the developments back home with requests that personal telephone conferences be had with certain senators and that the telegraph and mail
service be used to acquaint certain members with the necessity for a
tariff on oil.

Very soon an avalanche of communications began to arrive at
the senatorial offices. To those opposing the oil tariff proposal such
telephone calls, telegrams, special delivery letters, and what was
considered as propaganda mail were embarrassing especially since
the pending bill was considered to be a measure raising tariff rates
generally in order to protect American-made products from competition with the cheaper merchandise from abroad.

Because of developments and the embarrassment to some senators, the Senate investigating committee assumed jurisdiction and
began an investigation of the so-called "oil lobby." The active members of that early-day investigation committee were Senator T. H.
Caraway [D-Ark.][33] . . . , Senator Thomas J. Walsh [D-Mont.][34] . . . ,
and Senator John J. Blaine [R-Wis.].[35] . . .

The first act of the committee was to order its investigators to
make a raid on the headquarters of the oil delegation and to confis-
cate all mail, data, and documents that could be found. The raid
was made and the contents of the headquarters were collected,

sacked, and turned over to the Senate committee. Immediately thereafter the data confiscated was made available to the press and in addition one member of the committee, Senator Blaine, proceeded to fill the *Congressional Record* with copies of the data illegally confiscated.

At that point I protested the nature of the practices being followed and requested that the investigating committee hear Wirt Franklin, who was the chief spokesman for the delegation. I asked Mr. Franklin to prepare a statement explaining the reason for their mission to Washington, and on the date of the next committee meeting I appeared with the delegation chairman and personally requested that he be heard.

The committee, with three members present — Senators Caraway, Walsh, and Blaine — refused to permit Mr. Franklin to appear before the committee in order to explain the reasons for the presence of the citizen delegation in Washington to petition the Congress to provide relief for their oil industry. When the investigating committee refused to hear Wirt Franklin . . . , I concluded that the committee members were not interested in securing facts and information but rather they were seeking data to be used in opposing the oil tariff proposal. Acting on such conviction, I decided to present the matter directly to the Senate, and on Wednesday, March 19, 1930, I addressed the Senate at considerable length. For this presentation I shall use extracts only. . . .

"Mr. President, the amendment . . . embodies a request for a tariff on oil. More than that, it not only embodies a request for a tariff on oil but it involves a contest of oil against oil, a contest of domestic oil against foreign oil, a contest of independent oil against Standard Oil, and a contest of American oil against British oil. Every Senator upon this floor, when he comes to vote upon this question, must vote for oil; at that time he will have his choice of voting for American oil or for British oil, for independent oil or for Standard Oil, for domestic oil or foreign oil. . . .

"Mr. President, this issue here now raised is not alone whether this amendment should be agreed to; not alone whether the gigantic oil combines and mergers, some of them of foreign origin and foreign capital, should be taxed; not alone whether hundreds of thousands of American citizens should be helped, but the issue has assumed a larger and more important aspect, and we now have the question of whether citizens of the United States shall be denied the right to come to their own Capital, to confer with those in authority and to present petitions for redress of grievances. . . .

"On the day preceding the consideration of the petroleum amendment, Wirt Franklin, representing hundreds of thousands of oil-field workers, . . . was hailed before the lobby investigating committee and, before his examination was concluded, one member of the committee, in a speech on this floor, condemned him as an undesirable lobbyist. . . . After the petroleum amendment had been considered and passed upon on Friday and after the attack upon the accused, made here by the Senator from Wisconsin, a recessed session of the committee was held and at that time Mr. Franklin requested the committee to permit him to make a statement, which request was refused. . . .

"*The Evening Sun* of Baltimore likewise carried a first-page story under a bold heading. I have the paper here. The signed story contains the following: 'The most dazzlingly successful political maneuver of recent years was the surprise raid by the Caraway lobby committee on the headquarters of the Independent Oil Producers' Association late Thursday afternoon. At 4:00 Thursday afternoon, John Holland, investigator for the Caraway lobby committee, made his surprise raid on the oil headquarters located in the Mayflower Hotel.'

"*Labor*, a paper published here, the political and economic bible of thousands of workers in the country, said that the independent oil men 'might have won if the lobby investigating committee had not intervened.' On the same day the fight was waged the *Oklahoma*

City Times carried a front-page story under a heavy date line as follows: 'Late Thursday a subpoena was served on Franklin to appear Friday morning. Simultaneously, an investigator from the Senate committee appeared without warning and took possession of all of the letters, telegrams, and receipts in the office. No this isn't Russia.' . . . "

The fight for a tariff on oil was opposed by the importing companies and such companies, domestic and foreign, were the largest oil-producing, -refining, and -distributing companies in the world. The power of the national administration was enlisted in opposition to the relief sought by the smaller and independent individuals, associations, and corporations engaged in exploration, discovery, and production of oil; hence, it was an unequal fight that was waged when they sought relief and assistance at the hands of the Congress.

It has been said that no man is ever defeated until he knows that he cannot win. In my efforts to help my Oklahoma oil friends — land owners, drillers, operators, and managers — it never occurred to me that we would not win. At that stage of the development of the oil industry we had no department of the federal government that was charged with any responsibility respecting any phase of such industry. In presenting arguments and data in support of the relief requested we were forced to rely upon such statistics and facts as could be secured from current newspapers, magazines, and private reports of companies to their stockholders. In Senate debates we had no official data of any nature to present to support our position.

In outlining this effort to secure recognition for the masses engaged in the oil industry, it must be reported that the independent oil delegation had two powerful officials on their side, but under the circumstances such officials could do nothing other than to make suggestions and give advice as to matters of procedure. The two officials were Charles Curtis [R-Kans.],[36] the vice-president, and

Senator James E. Watson, [R-Ind.][37] . . . . Both were tariff supporters and both favored the tariff amendment but because of the determined opposition of the controlling and ruling powers in the administration, they were not able to assist publicly in the fight.

On one motion to add the oil amendment to the tariff bill, I missed by a single vote of securing a tie. The vice-president advised me personally to keep up the fight and suggested that I alter my amendment and re-submit it so as to have another try for success. He further suggested that if I could ever get a tie vote, as vice-president he would break such tie by casting his vote for such amendment.

Senator Watson, from my native state of Indiana, was my dependable friend at all times and in all matters save on purely political issues during the time he remained in the Senate. The further fact that I was a graduate of DePauw University, the senator's alma mater, did not injure my standing with the Senate Majority Leader at that time.

The weak point in our efforts was the fact that we did not have official information to back up our statements and arguments. The subcommittee appointed to hear the proponents of the tariff proposal did not have the testimony printed, so we were at a decided disadvantage in the fight on the Senate floor. Knowing the oil industry was an expanding and developing institution, and that very soon the government would no doubt become interested not only in the revenue which could be derived therefrom but in imposing restrictions, regulations, and controls over such industry, I decided to find a way to collect and assemble official information, data, and statistics to the end that when issues should arise relating to or affecting such industry the Congress would have such data available for consideration with problems that were certain to develop.

I suggested that the Senate appoint a special committee to look into and consider all phases of the oil industry with the sole purpose of securing all available data for the use and benefit of the

Congress. I hoped to prevent a reoccurrence of a lack of authentic if not official data if and when another oil problem should come before the Congress. . . .

After two years of the worst depression in history, and with an administration showing little interest in the welfare of the "common man," I continued to make efforts to secure consideration and assistance for the many unemployed in my state as well as in the other states of the Union. Early in March, as the Seventy-first Congress was coming to an end, I urged the Senate to pass Senate Resolution No. 418, which proposed the creating of a committee to study the oil industry, but each time I asked for action, objections were heard and such opposition meant delay and indefinite debate.

Knowing that the session had to end at noon on March 3rd, I intensified my efforts by occupying all available time in urging the Senate to take up and pass the oil resolution. I was under no illusion that I could do more than call the attention to the Congress and perhaps the country to the fact that while relief had been provided in the form of rebates to the larger taxpayers, and that through the enactment of the Reconstruction Finance Corporation, funds had been made available for loans to banks, railroads, and the large industrial organizations, yet nothing had been done to help the veterans, the unemployed, the farmers, and the small business concerns of the country.

On March 2nd, only one day away from adjournment, I took the floor with the intent of forcing passage of the oil resolution or speaking until the sine die adjournment of the Senate. I knew that I could prevent the passage of all legislation and also could prevent the confirmation of all pending appointments, and with such power, and knowing how to use it, I took chances on being able to secure an agreement for the passage of the resolution rather than to have all legislative business blocked.

The record shows that I held the floor on March 2nd until after midnight when Senator Watson, the Majority Leader, came to me while I was speaking and whispered that if I would yield to him he would move to recess until 9 o'clock on the following morning, March 3rd. I agreed to his proposal on condition that I should have the floor upon the reconvening of the Senate. . . .

Immediately after adjournment William Hard,[38] a prominent Washington columnist, reported the proceedings in the Senate over an NBC network, in part, as follows. . . . "The Senate this morning met at nine o'clock. Senator Thomas of Oklahoma resumed the floor. He had occupied it last night for several hours. It was still his. He was interested in pressing the passage of a resolution for an inquiry into the oil industry. He was encountering great opposition to it. He was having difficulty in securing a unanimous consent to the taking of a vote upon it. He was also experiencing a fear that, even if a vote should be had, the resolution, being a resolution which in his opinion was necessary in order to reveal the economic forces and the corporate interests responsible in his judgment for the deplorable distress existing in the oil districts of his state, would be defeated.

"In that mood Senator Thomas of Oklahoma, tall, spare-built, black-suited, white-haired, rose in his place in the back row of the Senate on the Democratic side, at the right hand of the presiding Vice President of the United States, at nine o'clock this morning. Much important legislation was pending unconcluded. The bill for federal assistance to maternity and infancy health and to general rural health awaited a vote. The resolution for the further legislative restriction of immigration awaited a vote. The bill for a revision of our copyright laws, after twelve years of controversy, awaited a vote. Numerous other measures, representing long labor and in some cases representing instant national need, awaited an opportunity of enactment.

"In these circumstances Senator Thomas, drawing himself up to his full physical height and to an even higher height of mental and moral determination to wreak vengeance upon his fellow-Senators who were opposing the oil resolution but who had resolutions and bills of their own for which they wished consideration, began to talk. He was implored to give way in order that measures with a genuine chance of legislative success might be debated. Except for veterans' hospitalization he declined.

"Senator Reed of Pennsylvania, the leader, in a sense, of the opposition to the oil resolution, sent word to Senator Thomas, offering to withdraw the opposition if Senator Thomas would consent to have the inquiry into the oil industry conducted not by a committee of Senators but by the Federal Trade Commission. Senator Reed understood Senator Thomas to reject this offer. Senator Reed accordingly continued the opposition to Senator Thomas's resolution proposal.

"Senator Thomas thereupon grasped firmly a certain pile of frayed and greasy rags which lay beside his desk and which he said were a pair of overalls. These overalls, he said, were a sad epitome and symbol of the destitute and desperate workmen of the western oil fields. He would talk, he said, on behalf of the kind of men who had to wear that kind of clothes.

"He looked from time to time at Senator Reed of Pennsylvania over on the Republican side of the Senate, near the center aisle, who, besides being interested in stopping Senator Thomas's oil idea, was interested also in forwarding and passing an idea of his own, in the form of a resolution, for drastically checking immigration during the next two years. Every minute consumed by Senator Thomas in oratory regarding oil was potentially a minute lost by Senator Reed for orating and voting on immigration. Senator Thomas realized it heartily. Senator Reed realized it bitterly. Senator Thomas's face became bland with consciousness of power. Senator Reed's face became flushed with consciousness of frustration. . . .

"Senator Thomas this morning, with occasional glances at his victim from Pennsylvania, talked from nine to nine-thirty and then from nine-thirty to ten and then from ten to ten-thirty, along about which time, if I remember the moments accurately, Senator George W. Norris of Nebraska rose from his place on the Republican side and walked over to the Democratic side and sat down a few desks away from Senator Thomas and began to regard him with looks of serene and at the same time animated pleasure. Senator Norris had begun to grasp the possibility that Senator Thomas might indeed persevere to the end in giving the country one of the most protracted and one of the most complete object-lessons it has ever had in the legislative wreckage that can be caused by a fixed congressional adjournment hour. . . .

"Encouraged by Senator Norris and unintimidated by Senator Reed, Senator Thomas talked from ten-thirty to eleven and then from eleven to eleven-thirty and then on till he ejaculated: 'Mr. President, the issue is joined at this last moment. We have two groups in this country. One is the special-interest group which is organized and which reigns. The other is the people's group which is unorganized and which is ruled. Mergers will presently give us a complete industrial monopoly, and a complete industrial monopoly will give us complete human slavery. Mr. President, it is now eleven o'clock and fifty-eight minutes.' Having made that announcement, and having thus reminded himself that he needed to exert himself for only two minutes more, Senator Thomas relaxed, and descended from the peaks of national vision and prophecy. . . . "

The next day after the final adjournment of the Congress, the *Tulsa World*, one of the leading newspapers of the southwest, printed the following editorial: "Senator Thomas of Oklahoma is temporarily the most talked-of man in the United States. His filibuster in behalf of the independent oil industry was deliberate, but it had spectacular features which will cause him to be reprobated in some quarters, praised in others and rather generally respected as daring and determined. Doubtless he aroused antagonisms which will last quite a while and appear against him at strategic times hereafter.

"Ordinarily *The World* deplores filibusters, particularly at the last

hour, when many things besides the subject of filibuster are at stake.
But if a filibuster ever was justified, this one was. The Senator was
fair, after he had seized a strategic advantage and tied the Senate in
a knot, in stopping to give the relentless opposition a chance to vote
upon the resolution of inquiry into the oil business. Twice his offer
was refused by desperate standpatters. Senator Thomas doubtless
argued to himself that the oil industry in several great states, the
business in which untold millions are invested and in which a great
many thousands of people are employed and under which a very
important part of the United States has been built up, was more
important than anything else the Senate could consider in its closing hours. . . . It is very likely Senator Thomas's filibuster will
force — at the next session of Congress — some serious and intel-
ligent consideration of the oil crisis. . . ."

As predicted in the editorial and as hoped for by myself, we did
not have to await the next session of the Congress for favorable
action at the hands of the government. The record shows that immediately upon the adjournment of the Congress, President Hoover recognized the oil industry by calling a conference of those
interested to meet at Colorado Springs, Colorado. . . . The conference was held and I am pleased to reflect that from that date to
the present time the all important oil industry has had full recognition and cooperation by the government at Washington.

A Prophecy That Came True
The Man in Overalls

The paramount issue of Thirty-two,
    Says Senator Elmer Thomas,
Is not the fate of the favored few
    Or the barons of trade and commerce,
But the future of that grim son of toil
    On whom the country calls
To hew its wood and plough its soil —
    The man in overalls.

The Oklahoman makes a plea
   For one too oft forgot,
Who bows his back and bends his knee
   And serves in lowly lot;
The labor that white-collars shirk
   Upon his shoulders falls,
'Tis he who does the world's real work —
   This man in overalls.

He sends no one to Capitol Hill
   To lobby his own laws,
He stays at home to tug and till
   And do the nation's chores;
Of all the agents slick that swarm
   Thru House and Senate halls,
There's none who wears the uniform
   Of the man in overalls.

Tho' it be tattered, patched and torn
   And soiled by Mother Earth,
He boasts an honored garb that's worn
   By hearts of noblest worth;
A symbol now of want and pain
   And misery that appalls,
This issue of the next campaign
   Is the man in overalls!

The above verses were written by George Sanford Holmes[39] immediately after hearing the speech delivered in the Senate just prior to the final adjournment of the Seventy-first Congress at 12 o'clock noon, March 3, 1931. . . .

PLAN TO RELIEVE DEPRESSION:
MY PARAMOUNT ACCOMPLISHMENT

The Great Depression descended upon the United States in the fall of 1929. The cause of the collapse of the American economy has never been satisfactorily explained; hence, instead of spending

time in trying to find the reason or reasons for the panic, I shall
relate my efforts in finding a way out of the economic chaos into
which our people had found themselves. . . .

The results of such depression were many and no one escaped.
The stock and commodity markets collapse pointed the way to what
was to follow. Prices of everything tumbled and the people, for the
want of money, ceased to make purchases. Immediately the slump
was felt by retail merchants, then in turn by jobbers, wholesalers,
and factories. Activities in communication and transportation, of
necessity, declined. Unemployment increased rapidly and all engaged in the professions suffered for the want of patronage.

The slowdown of business was not brought about by a scarcity of
any class of raw materials, for there was an abundance of everything. The trouble was that the people had lost their buying power.
Farmers could not sell their products for enough to pay costs of
production, so they had no money with which to buy the things they
actually needed. Factories were not receiving orders for their output, so they were forced to lay off their employees. Each group of
people and each class of industry affected and reacted upon each
and every other group and class and, within a few months, the work
of the country was almost at a standstill. The wage earners desiring
to pay their taxes and to meet their bills bid against each other for
such few jobs as were available; hence, wages fell. Farmers had to
sell whatever they possessed to get funds to pay their debts so that
markets and stockyards were flooded and prices fell to the lowest
level in generations. Because of a falling price level the value of
property became unstable and, under such conditions, banks not
only refused to make new loans but began trying to collect their
loans outstanding. The nationwide American panic expanded to
other countries so that by mid-1931 the depression practically covered the entire world.

The first session of the Seventy-second Congress convened in
December 1931, and on the 8th of that month, President Hoover

sent his message to the Congress wherein, among other things, he said: "Within two years there have been revolutions or acute social disorders in nineteen countries, embracing more than half the population of the world. Ten countries have been unable to meet their external obligations. In fourteen countries, embracing a quarter of the world's population, former monetary standards have been temporarily abandoned. In a number of countries there have been acute financial panics or compulsory restraints upon banking." In order to help the nations indebted to our government, the president said: "Upon the initiative of this Government a year's postponement of reparations and other inter-governmental debts was brought about."

With respect to bank failures, the president reported: "One phase of the credit situation is indicated in the banks. During the past year banks, representing 3 percent of our total deposits, have been closed. A large part of these failures has been caused by withdrawals for hoarding, as distinguished from the failures early in the depression where weaknesses due to mismanagement were the larger cause of failure. Despite their closing, many of them will pay in full. Although such withdrawals have practically ceased, yet $1,000,000,000 of currency was previously withdrawn which has still to return to circulation."

With respect to the effect of the depression, President Hoover reported as follows: "The continuing credit paralysis has operated to accentuate the deflation and liquidation of commodities, real estate, and securities below any reasonable basis of values. All of this tends to stifle business, especially the smaller units, and finally expresses itself in further depression of prices and values, in restriction on new enterprise, and in increased unemployment." After reporting on conditions . . . , the president said: "I am opposed to any direct or indirect government dole. The breakdown and increased unemployment in Europe is due in part to such practices. Our people are providing against distress from unemployment in true American fashion by a magnificent response to public appeal and by action of local governments."

The Congress gave consideration to the message and the recommendations made therein but nothing was done, and conditions, instead of improving, became progressively worse. The stock, security, and commodity markets remained open but only to record falling prices. In some states wheat was selling for 20 cents per bushel; corn for 15 cents; cotton for 5 cents per pound; and hogs and beef cattle were plentiful at 3 dollars per hundred weight.

At that time the farm population numbered some 30 million or about one-fourth of our total population. The number of unemployed was estimated to be some 15 million, so that the farmers and wage earners together, with their families and dependents, made up almost 100 million of our total population. Representing, in part, as I did, an agricultural state with many thousands of wage earners, I knew that conditions were intolerable and that the government should make an effort to relieve the distress that existed among the people.

During the Hoover administration I was one of the new members of the Senate and, in addition, was a member of the minority party. Because of such facts my opportunities for making suggestions and securing consideration for my proposals were exceedingly limited. New senators can draw their salaries, answer correspondence, attend committee and Senate sessions; prepare and introduce bills; make speeches; cast votes and report to their constituents their plans for solving public problems; and such list of activities embraces about all that they may accomplish during the early years of their services. Nevertheless, they can try to find solutions to pending problems. If they are successful in securing the facts and are able to properly analyze such data and thereafter prepare a real remedy for the problem, they have every opportunity of securing recognition. If they persist they will sooner or later meet with success. . . .

Among the many proposals for relief, two were given major consideration: [first], to provide assistance through a vast program of public works; and, second, to increase prices of commodities and properties through the exercise of the constitutional power to regulate the value of the dollar downward. The program for public works was to provide immediate jobs for the millions out of employment, and the monetary plan was to gradually raise the general price level through a process of cheapening the dollar.

In as much as the value of the dollar controls price, it was obvious that in order to increase prices it was necessary to decrease the value of the monetary unit. In order for the Congress to exercise its constitutional power to regulate the value of the dollar downward, a number of specific things were necessary to be performed, and under the Hoover administration, because of opposition, not one of the necessary acts was possible of performance.

The Federal Reserve Board could have brought relief but being influenced, if not controlled, by the administration in power, it failed to perform. The board had apparently already forgotten how it had reduced prices by some 50 percent immediately after World War One. . . . Because of reasons yet unexplained, the board failed to either act itself or to recommend legislation to the Congress. Willingly or unwillingly the board followed the announced policy of the administration.

President Hoover had announced in his message to the Congress that he was "opposed to any direct or indirect government dole," which declaration shaped the public policy during the remainder of the Seventy-second Congress. In the same message the president had likewise announced that "we have enormous volumes of idle money in the banks and in hoarding" and that "we do not require more money or working capital. . . ."

By the latter declaration the president served notice that he would not be agreeable to any program that would place more money in circulation. At that time, December 1931, there was a total of $4,821,000,000 in circulation with less than $1 billion of all kinds of real money—gold, silver, paper, and subsidiary coins—in the vaults of all the banks of the country.

At the same time, the total deposits in all the reporting banks was less than $50 billion, such deposits being 98 percent credit money, leaving only some 2 percent in gold, silver, currency, and minor coins. Statistics show that in 1932 the total farm income fell to some $6 billion and the total income of all the people was less than $40 billion. The general price level index number at that time was approximately 70 and the dollar value was $1.50. Such statistics meant that the price level was too low, caused by the dollar value being too high.

After World War One, the Federal Reserve Board[40] had reduced prices by restricting credits and taking out of circulation almost $2 billion of real money. If restricting credits and reducing the circulation of real money had the effect of reducing the price level from 154.4 in 1920 down to 96.7 in 1922, then it would seem that a reverse policy would have increased prices in 1929–32. However, neither a program for public works nor for raising prices was possible under the Hoover administration. The result of four years of government— 1929 to 1933 —was no relief for the people; a partial collapse of government; a general collapse of business; and the defeat of the party in power.

As the records show, the depression came unannounced, late in 1929, and within one year, adverse economic conditions confronted all save those with incomes from fixed investments. . . . In June of 1931, conferences were being held throughout the central and southwestern states in order to try to develop a plan for relief of the public generally. While the president was unwilling to aid the unemployed and was opposed to any program for increasing prices, yet he was favorable to granting a moratorium to the governments owing the United States vast sums of money.

On June 24, 1931, the Oklahoma State Chamber of Commerce

was host to delegates representing the Southwestern Trade Conference and to such conference I had been invited. During the
deliberations of the delegates I received a message from President
Hoover suggesting the advisability of granting a moratorium to England, France, and the other nations that owed us money. Whereupon, I took the liberty of reading the telegram to the conference.
After discussion and at my request, a committee was appointed to
prepare a statement setting forth the reaction of the delegates.

Personally, I was opposed to any postponement of the payment
of the debts due our government, but realizing that the administration had already decided to grant relief to the foreign governments,
and in the hope that by going along on a policy that was to be
carried out anyway I might be able to secure consideration of some
of our recommendations, I agreed to wire the president. . . . On July
1, 1931, I addressed a [similar] letter to my state governor, the
Honorable Wm. H. Murray.[41] . . . "It is conceded that unemployment will be with us the coming winter and many doubt if funds can
be raised for the Red Cross or other charitable organizations, with
which to give relief. A state-wide meeting is to be held at ten o'clock
A.M., July 6th, at Labor Temple, Oklahoma City, to consider plans
for taking care of the coming situation. The problem is a national
one, hence should be financed by the Federal Government. It is
proposed to inaugurate a vast internal improvement program to be
financed by federal funds to afford labor employment. Such a policy will accomplish the following purposes: First, it will secure improvements which will be made in natural course within the near
future; second, such improvements can be secured at reasonable
cost; and, third the program will afford employment for all who may
be in need. If the state-wide convention adopts the proposal or
program, a mid-western or interstate conference will be held, and
if such interstate convention is a success a national convention is
contemplated. . . ."

The state mass meeting was held as planned and, as recom-

Shortly after he took office as Oklahoma governor in 1931, William H.
Murray (center) welcomes Senator Thomas (left) and newly elected
senator Thomas P. Gore (right). Courtesy Western History Collections,
University of Oklahoma Libraries.

mended, an interstate conference was called to meet at Memphis, Tennessee. . . . The Memphis inter-state conference was well attended and strong resolutions were prepared and sent to President Hoover, advocating the creation of a vast public works program in order to provide jobs for the unemployed.

After intensive study of the situation covering trips to many parts of the country, I became convinced that while public works would offer temporary relief, it would require bold major policies to check the existing deflation and bring about better times. At the time, I was certain that only a trend of increasing prices would serve to bring any degree of hope to the people. While I was urging a program of public works and the payment of the soldier's bonus in cash, I had in mind that either or both of said proposals would not only provide quick temporary relief but would, through placing additional money in circulation, bring about the cheapening of the dollar and the consequent increase of prices. . . .

On more than one occasion in the Senate, I had suggested to the leaders of the then majority party that unless they changed their policy and program they would soon become a dwindling and weak minority. Although not a prophet, my guess and forecast came true. Within seven years thereafter the Republican membership in the Senate dwindled from 51 in 1929 to 27 in 1936, and 4 of the 27 were registered as Progressive, Independent, or Farmer Labor.

Early in my service in the Congress, I became convinced that the major wealth of the United States was massed back of the Republican Party. Acting on such conviction I accepted every invitation and opportunity of journeying to the larger cities in the hope that the industrial and financial leaders might be influenced to join in an effort to bring the depression to an end.

As an example of the meetings held on February 6, 1933, one month prior to the inauguration of Franklin D. Roosevelt as president, I had the opportunity of addressing a large group at the

Waldorf-Astoria hotel in New York City. The group was made up of bankers and members of the New York Stock Exchange; the Curb; and the cotton, coffee, sugar, raw silk, and maritime exchanges.

To the members I spoke on the subject Face the Facts, as follows: "We are now in the forty-first month of the worst depression in history. While all know of the effects, yet practically no two agree as to either the cause of or the remedy for the economic and personal distress now existing among our people. . . . As a member of the policy-making branch of the Government, and one who has been in many parts of the United States during the past few months, I come to New York, the Nation's metropolis, to present the facts and to reason with you — you, and you alone, who can give the order and set in motion the machinery which will check the downward trend and start the greatest, strongest, and richest nation of the earth upward toward economic and human recovery.

"What are the conditions today? Millions are unemployed, trade is stagnated, business is paralyzed, taxes are in arrears, interest is in default, law is ignored, and individuals, corporations, cities, counties, states, and the Federal Government are using the Nation's credit with which to pay taxes, interest, and to meet the overhead and running expenses of our several organizations.

"Why are conditions thus? Why are our people, corporations, cities, counties, and states forced to borrow from the Government? The answer: Because there are no other institutions or agencies able or willing to extend such credit. Why are the regular institutions and agencies unable or unwilling to take care of such demands? The answer: Because our people, our institutions, our municipalities, and our states are without income and ability to meet their existing obligations, and therefore are not good risks for further credit. When will conditions improve? The answer: When the people regain buying power, when the unemployed have jobs, and when farmers have cost of production — then will trade be revived, taxes and interest will be paid, value will re-enter commodities, farms, and factories, and the prosperity we once knew will again return. . . .

"What is the cause of existing and growing distress? It would seem that we have everything necessary to make a people prosperous, contented, and happy. We have the richest, strongest, and most influential Nation of the earth. We have almost one-half the monetary gold of the world. We have a magnificently developed country. We have food, clothing, and merchandise in abundance; and we have an industrious, ambitious, and a patient people — but something is wrong, something is missing, a cog in our economic machinery is worn, damaged, or destroyed. . . .

"Gentlemen of New York, face the facts. Sound business and prosperity increase in proportion as sound money and credit expand. At the risk of boredom permit me for a moment to indulge in figures. In 1912 the amount of money in circulation was three and one-third billion dollars. From 1912 to 1921 the money in circulation increased from three and one-third to six and one-half billion dollars. In 1920, with the greatest amount of money ever in circulation, we had the highest prices and the best times in history.

"In 1920 influential powers decided that prices were too high and such powers, sometimes wise, decided to bring down or cheapen prices by increasing the value of the dollar. This was done by withdrawing money from circulation, thereby making money scarce, and at the same time increasing its purchasing power. The program was inaugurated. One-third of the money of the people was withdrawn from circulation. Deflation was in progress. The value of the dollar went up, and the prices of commodities, farm lands, real estate, and property generally tumbled. The plan from the viewpoint of its powerful sponsors worked. It was a complete success, and today we have the highest valued dollar and the consequent lowest prices in history.

"Wheat is the lowest priced ever; hogs and livestock the lowest in a century; and other commodity prices and property values generally low in proportion; and yet these powerful influences responsible for this economic crime and tragedy seem to wonder why our economic structure is near collapse. If increasing the volume of money in circulation from 1912 to 1920 was responsible for the general increase in commodity prices and values; and if from 1921 to 1933 the decrease of the currency and the destruction of credit were responsible for the general fall in prices, then why are we not justified in concluding that a reversal of the present policy of deflation would bring an end to the present depression and start the Nation on the upturn toward economic recovery and prosperity?

"With conditions as they are today, it is not a question of whether we want to check deflation — not whether such check is desirable — but the demand is mandatory that an end to deflation be brought about and at once. Even an end to deflation will not suffice. The dollar has value and buying power which it cannot retain if the poise, peace, and equilibrium of our people are to be maintained.

"In support of this conclusion, I direct your attention to the following facts: From the most reliable estimates we must concede that the total massed debts of the people amount to at least two hundred billion dollars. Most of this indebtedness was contracted immediately prior to, during, and immediately after 1920, and at a time when the value of the dollar ranged from 40 to 60 cents.

"Today we cannot liquidate this indebtedness with 50-cent dollars, not even with 100-cent dollars, but to get rid of these bonds, notes, mortgages, and installments, we must pay with 160-cent dollars. Hence it must be plain that instead of the people owing massed debts in the sum of two hundred billion dollars, they must earn, save, and pay value to the extent of three hundred twenty billion dollars to liquidate such indebtedness. . . .

"I next call your attention to the tax burden of the Nation. It costs the people annually some five billion dollars to run the Federal Government. It costs the people of the states, cities, counties, and districts annually some seven billion dollars more to pay their local expenses; hence, the people must earn and pay each year some twelve billion dollars to meet their tax obligations.

"But can they pay with twelve billion dollars of value? Most certainly they cannot. Instead of being able to pay with twelve billion dollars of value they must pay in 160-cent dollars, which, when computed, forces the people to part with wealth in the total sum of 19.2 billion dollars to meet their annual tax bills. If this analysis and interpretation are correct, do you still wonder why taxes are not being paid? . . .

"The people are not paying their taxes, and they are not paying their interest and their debts, because they are unable to secure these high-priced dollars with which to meet their obligations. To demand and insist that they meet a 50-cent obligation with a dollar and a half payment is nothing short of oppression, rapacity, and extortion. . . .

"Is there no relief, help, and aid possible for the people of the country? Relief, to be worthy the name, must go further than Federal loans and doles to industry, the states, counties, cities, and even to the people of the Nation. Relief in the form of loans and doles only postpones the day of economic death. Relief, to be of benefit, must mean employment, must mean cost of production, and must mean expanding and growing purchasing power in the hands and pockets of the masses of the people of the country.

"Can such relief be provided! Reason with me for an additional moment! If the expansion of the currency and credit from 1912 to 1920 caused a general increase in commodity and property prices, and if the deflation of the currency and credit from 1920 to 1930 caused a general decline in commodity and property prices, then who can deny that a reversal of the present policy of deflation and the inauguration of reasonable and controlled expansion of currency and credit would bring an up-turn in business and resultant hope in countless millions now on the verge of despair? . . .

"If conditions are as represented, and if such conditions have been brought about in whole or in part by a manipulation of money and credit, then who is responsible for what President Hoover concedes to be the 'worst depression in history'? Under the Constitution the Congress, and only the Congress, can coin money and regulate its value. This responsibility is fixed. The power abides inherently and exclusively in the policy-making branch of the Government; but from a practical standpoint the Congress is either unable or unwilling to assert and exercise such specially conferred and expressed constitutional power.

"Notwithstanding the plain mandate of the Constitution, as a rule, financial policies do not originate with the Congress. As a rule, they do not even originate in Washington. When I stated a few moments ago that 'you,' and you alone, can give the order and set in motion the machinery which will pull us out of the mire, I meant that the financial policies of America originate right here in this great city.

"The New York Federal Reserve Bank[42] is the head and heart dominating and controlling the fiscal policies of our Government. Working and cooperating with this financial institution are the great banks of New York City. The policies of these banks are supposed to be controlled by the wisest financial brains of the Nation, and such control, as might be expected, is exercised always in the interests of the stockholders of such institutions. The heads of these powerful banks, together with their economic and financial advisors, have, as a practical proposition, Washington and the Congress as their agents.

"Today the Government at Washington is only one of the clients of this unified and powerful financial aggregation. A nod and a whisper by the powers mentioned can turn the tide and reverse the processes of deflation and depression. The longer the signal is delayed the more terrible the penalty now certain to be inflicted. The people forming the cities, counties, states, and even the Federal

Government are bankrupt and prostrate. Because of their condition moratoriums are being declared and enforced. Judges are silent, the law is impotent, and the tide of resentment and condemnation is sweeping westward across the continent. In conclusion, if the present financial policies are not altered; if deflation is not checked; if the people are not to be permitted to even have a chance to retain their property — a chance to pay their honest debts, then a new issue will arise — the form, extent, and result of which cannot now be foretold. . . ."

In waging the campaign for higher prices through a reduction of the value of the dollar, I accepted invitations and presented my plan to numerous groups. . . . Along with formal meetings, I had many private dinners and conferences similar to the one arranged for me in New York City in January 1932. The dinner was given by a number of the leading bankers and businessmen of the city. Among those present were Charles Mitchell, president of the National City Bank; Albert Wiggin, chairman, and Charles McCain, president of the Chase National Bank; George Harrison, governor of the Federal Reserve Bank of New York; Benjamin Anderson; Mortimer Buckner; Joseph Maxwell; Charles Hayden; Robert Harriss; and Randolph Burgess.[43] . . .

In my efforts to secure support for a program to increase prices, I sought information and advice from every person whom I thought was competent and perhaps willing to assist in the undertaking. In company with Senator Burton K. Wheeler [D-Mont.][44] . . . we were entertained at dinner with a few other guests at the home of Winthrop W. Aldrich,[45] chairman of the board of the Chase National Bank in New York City. As at other similar conferences the subject of money, prices, and the depression was discussed and various plans were suggested to check the deflation and to reverse the trend from depression to a return of prosperity.

We found the bankers almost universally opposed to the plans we suggested. They opposed any reduction in the weight of the gold dollar; opposed the wider use of silver; opposed any increase in the issuance of Treasury notes; opposed the development of a public works program; and . . . opposed to the payment of the bonus to veterans. It seemed that the only program that they would support was a balancing of the budget through a reduction of appropriations. At that time — 1932 — the total annual income was approximately $40,000,000,000; the total federal receipts were $1,924,000,000; and the total expenditures were $4,659,000,000.

With such a low national income it was clear to me that appropriations could not possibly be reduced sufficiently to come within our income; hence, the only possible solution was to increase prices so that the people could produce at a profit. . . . In addition to many speeches on the Senate floor and to groups away from Washington, I had invitations to prepare statements and articles for newspapers, the press services, and magazines. . . . The foregoing activities were in addition to my regular and constant advocacy of money relief in the Senate. Long before 1932, I realized that there could be no relief secured for the common man at the hands of either the Seventy-first or Seventy-second Congresses. However, I persisted in the hope that something might happen to alter the viewpoint of the administration and the Congress. . . .

While the Constitution confers upon the Congress exclusive jurisdiction and power to regulate the value of money, I learned that such power had never been used. It is true that the weight of the gold dollar had been changed twice during President Andrew Jackson's administration. In each instance the purpose was not "to regulate the value of money," but instead to try to bring the gold and silver dollars into an exact parity with each other. The demonetization of silver in 1873 had for its purpose not the regulation of the value of money but instead to get rid of silver as a primary monetary metal and thereby establish gold as the single standard for not only the United States but to assist in making gold the standard for the moneys of the world. The act of March 14, 1900, was not passed to regulate the value of the dollar, but instead merely to officially declare and establish the gold dollar as the standard United States dollar. . . .

At the end of the Hoover administration the Norris (Lame Duck) amendment [which set inauguration in January following the November election] had not been approved, so the new president was not inaugurated until March 4, 1933. The people had voted in favor of a change in administration . . . . [but] in the absence of any relief, times grew progressively worse. The *Saturday Evening Post*, in a special article entitled "The Origins of the Banking Panic of March 4, 1933," published on June 8, 1935, referred to conditions existing during the month of February, immediately preceding the inauguration of Franklin D. Roosevelt, as follows: "The developments during the first two weeks of February had transformed mere apprehension into fear all over the country. The withdrawal of currency and gold for hoarding had increased from about $5,000,000 a day at the first of February to $15,000,000 a day by the middle of the month. All the phenomena so well known in European experience antecedent to an abandonment of or change in the gold standard both appeared and grew. . . . "

Continuing, the article related: " . . . The intention of the incoming administration appeared in public print in a press dispatch of January 30, 1933, and this was promptly emphasized by being read before the Senate by Senator Thomas of Oklahoma, who said: 'I desire at this point to call the attention of the Senate to a news item that appears in today's *Washington Herald*. . . . While the President-elect was represented as being open-minded on the proper plans to adopt, he was said to be prepared to accept some form of currency inflation in order to raise commodity prices and ease the financial stringency of the Nation. He still is studying the question. This issue has been dinned into the ears of Roosevelt by both Democratic and Progressive partisans. . . . ' "

Now it can be stated definitely that President Roosevelt offered

In this 1934 political cartoon, James Farley welcomes Upton Sinclair to the "Democratic Club." Seated in the club are several well-known Democrats, including Elmer Thomas, Carter Glass, Huey Long, Al Smith, Hiram Johnson, and Joseph Robinson. A former Socialist, Sinclair was now the Democratic candidate in the California gubernatorial campaign. Courtesy Carl Albert Center Congressional Archives, University of Oklahoma.

the Treasury portfolio to Senator Carter Glass[46] of Virginia, and that such cabinet position was refused for the obvious reason that the senator was apprehensive that the new administration was seriously considering the regulation of the value of money downward. The record shows conclusively that the vast majority of the financial and business interests of the United States, including the leaders of the Republican administration, the Federal Reserve System, the large insurance companies, . . . and such influential figures in the Democratic Party as Bernard M. Baruch and Carter Glass were opposed to any attempt to regulate the value of the dollar downward in order to raise prices and thereby reinvest commodities and property and value. It was in the face of such adverse recommendations and the opposition of the Republican leadership, together with like opposition from the ultra conservative forces in the Democratic Party, that I had to wage almost a one-man fight to secure economic relief for our people, as well as for our government.

At the end of the Hoover administration all banks were closed; fifteen million men were unemployed, trade was stagnated, business was paralyzed, smokestacks were smokeless, dinner pails were empty, taxes were unpaid, interest was in default, and incipient revolutions were wide-spread. Individuals, corporations, counties, cities, and most of the states were accepting doles from the government, which in effect placed such individuals, corporations, and municipal subdivisions in the federal bread line.

On March 4, 1933, Franklin D. Roosevelt was inaugurated president of the United States. . . . Soon after the Congress convened [in special session] the president sent a message recommending legislation to aid agriculture. In such message the president said: "At the same time that you and I are joining in emergency action to bring order to our banks, and to make our regular Federal expenditures balance our income, I deem it of equal importance to take other and similar steps without waiting for a later meeting of the Congress. One of these is of definite, constructive importance to our economic recovery. It relates to agriculture and seeks to increase the purchasing power of our farmers."

Immediately upon receipt of the message the two houses of the Congress began holding hearings to determine just what legislation to recommend for passage. The House developed and passed a bill (H.R. 3835) and sent same to the Senate. The bill, as passed by the House, was known as the "Agricultural Adjustment Act." When the bill reached the Senate it was referred to the Committee on Agriculture and Forestry, of which I was a member on the majority side. I gave the measure my support but frankly advised the committee that if the measure was held constitutional and if it produced the results claimed for it, such results would be of no substantial benefit to the 30 million farmers of the United States. I suggested that we recommend bold and direct action "to increase the purchasing power of our farmers" as had been recommended by the president.

My plan to increase agricultural and all prices was the result of a study of the money question since the Bryan "Free Silver" campaign in 1896. Early in my consideration of money and its effect upon prices, I became convinced that the value of the dollar controls prices and that prices control income and prosperity. It is obvious that high-valued money causes prices to be low and that low-valued money causes prices to be high. . . .

At the beginning of the Roosevelt administration every bank in the United States was closed. It required an examination and a certificate of solvency prior to the reopening of each of the closed banks. All this meant that people were skeptical of banks and such money as was outside the Treasury—in circulation—was either in closed banks or was hoarded. Thus, the scarce money made the dollar valuable and the high-valued dollar caused prices to fall to the lowest level in decades.

The problem confronting President Roosevelt in early 1933 was exactly opposite to the problem that confronted President Warren G. Harding in early 1921. President Harding wanted to lower prices and accomplished the end desired by making money scarce; hence, it was my plan to increase prices by making money more plentiful. I submitted my program to the Agricultural Committee and while the members were sympathetic to the plan, they decided that they did not have jurisdiction over money; hence, they voted against the acceptance of my money amendment as part of the Agricultural Adjustment Act.

Being convinced that I had the solution to the low prices di-
lemma, I moved that the committee include in its report on the bill
a statement with respect to the necessity for monetary adjustment
in order to check the deflation and to restore prices to a normal
level. While the committee refused to accept my monetary amendment, it did approve my motion by a vote of 16 to 0, and the report
on the bill contained . . . a statement as to the necessity of an expansion of the currency and the absolute necessity for an increase in
commodity prices. The statement as prepared and adopted by the
committee follows . . . "Agriculture demands that the farmer should
have a 100-cent dollar; that the purchasing power of the dollar
should be fixed and established at that point to serve the best interests of the people, trade, commerce, and industry; and that when
such value is once fixed it should be stabilized at such value. We
report further that no just, substantial, reliable, or permanent relief
can be provided agriculture or any other industry until the money
question is considered and adjusted."

The farm bill was reported to the Senate calendar on April 5, and
was taken up for consideration on the Senate floor very soon thereafter. When the bill (H.R. 3835) was placed before the Senate and
made the unfinished business, I introduced my money amendment, had it printed, and made ready to be offered for consideration at the proper time. Under the Senate rules all committee
amendments must be disposed of before it is in order to offer an
individual's amendments.

The general debate on the bill consumed a few days and during
such time I sent a printed copy of the amendment to President
Roosevelt. On April 22, the president acknowledged receipt of the
amendment. . . . At about the time the president sent me the note
acknowledging receipt of the amendment, he sent word that he
wanted to talk to me about the amendment. An hour was fixed for
the conference, when I appeared at the White House, where the
provisions of the bill were discussed.

Two points respecting the amendment appealed to the president. One was that the powers proposed to be conferred on the chief executive would, if exercised properly, increase prices. And, two, with such powers in his hand he would be free to act without further legislation by the Congress. . . . While I did not choose the time for the conference, such time was perfect for my appearance before the president. I knew that the president was very greatly interested in the International Monetary Conference which was soon to meet in London. . . . During our conference I casually suggested that if the amendment was adopted and became the law that he would have all power over money and that with such powers he would be able to definitely agree to, if not dictate, terms at the London conference without having to make treaties which would have to be brought back, presented to, and ratified by the United States Senate, whose membership in the main know little about the intricacies of the science of money. The London meeting was to be largely a monetary conference; hence, when such suggestion was made I knew that I did not need to present any additional arguments in order to secure administration approval of and support for the plan to raise the general level of prices, which of course would include farm prices.

The basic theory of the amendment was to provide a plan or plans for increasing the money in circulation. It was and is known to all students of money that an increase in circulation of money units increases prices. To secure an increase of prices, different plans were suggested by different groups and interests. For example, the representatives from the silver-producing states advocated a wider use of silver, through remonetization, as a means of expanding the circulation.

Another group favored an increase in the circulation through a decrease in the weight of the standard gold dollar. . . . At that time we had over $4 billion in gold, so that if each dollar had been cut into two equal parts and each part had been declared by law to be one dollar, then such a program would have added some $4 billion to the circulation and prices would have been increased thereby.

A third sizeable group insisted that we could and should print and issue into circulation Treasury notes to whatever extent necessary to raise the price level to the 1926 level, or in other words to give the dollar a 100-cent value as measured by the Bureau of Labor Statistics price index. Still, the more conservative members of the Congress, realizing that something should be done to raise prices, indicated that they would not seriously oppose an effort to raise prices through open market operations carried out by the Federal Reserve Board. The final vote on the amendment disclosed that there was in the Senate a number of members who were opposed to any and all plans for raising the then prevailing low general price level.

My long study of the money question and my experience in drafting and presenting legislation enabled me to analyze the facts and to develop a bill which would command the maximum support in the Senate and House of Representatives. . . . Knowing that I had to secure at least a majority of each house to support the amendment, I prepared the legislation with such end in view. While several of the plans proposed, if properly administered, would have produced an increase in prices, yet I knew that if only one plan was suggested, each of the other plans would be offered either as substitutes or as additional programs to accomplish the end all supporters had in mind; hence, in order to secure the maximum support, I joined all of the plans for increasing the circulation in one amendment and then proposed to leave the exact plan or plans to be used to the discretion of the president.

I knew that if I could prepare a bill, or an amendment to the farm bill, that would enlist the support and votes of the proponents of the several plans that had been suggested, [then] in the absence of any other relief program I could secure favorable action in both houses of the Congress. At that time I did not know just how the new president would react to the plan to stop the deflation and, at the same time, to change the trend to one of increasing prices; hence, it was deemed necessary to convince President Roosevelt that something should be done and done at once to arrest the ravages of the almost four-year-old depression.

Senator Wheeler of Montana was the outstanding leader of the strong and numerous group favoring the expansion of the circulation through a proposal to remonetize silver. In the latter days of the Hoover administration Senator Wheeler made a special fight for silver and at all times he was active in advocating a program to re-establish silver as one of our primary and basic money metals. On January 25, 1932, the senator addressed the Senate at considerable length in explaining and advocating the passage of a bill he had just introduced proposing to remonetize silver. At a later date Senator Wheeler offered his silver bill as an amendment to a measure under consideration on the Senate floor and secured more than one-third of the members present at that time.

The specific thing that I was trying to accomplish was to secure a reduction in the value or buying power of the dollar. I was certain that I was acting under the authority of the federal Constitution wherein it is provided in Section 8 of Article I that "[t]he Congress shall have power . . . to coin money" and to "regulate the value thereof. . . . " Hence, any plan or program that would regulate the value of the dollar downward was acceptable to me. . . . The amendment, as developed, contained the plans or devices to accomplish the end I had in view, and at the same time the different plans were together supported by approximately two-thirds of the membership of each of the two houses of the Congress. . . .

After my conference at the White House, it was definitely understood that the plan to raise the general price level through an adjustment and regulation of the value of the dollar downward was approved and all branches of the executive department obviously were requested to cooperate in having such plan added to and made a part of the then pending farm bill. The fact that the amendment had not at that time been presented to and considered by the Banking and Currency Committee made it necessary, for orderly procedure, that I withdraw such amendment from the Senate and have it referred to such committee for consideration and report. That course was followed and within hours the hearing was held. Secretary William Woodin[47] of the Treasury Department and his staff of experts appeared in support of the proposal, whereupon the committee instructed its chairman, Senator Duncan Fletcher [D-Fla.],[48] to report the amendment back to the Senate with a recommendation that it be approved as an amendment to the pending farm bill. . . .

The members of the Federal Reserve Board were not consulted when the original text of the amendment was being prepared, for the obvious reason that on February 21, 1933, the board had called in the Federal Reserve Advisory Council, made up of leading bankers from each of the twelve Federal Reserve districts, and had such council pass a resolution calling upon President Roosevelt to issue a public statement setting forth his position with respect to currency and credit expansion. The council, in effect, demanded that President Roosevelt declare a policy of balancing the budget through a reduction of expenditures and against either currency or credit expansion.[49]

The chairman of the advisory committee transmitted the resolution to the president-elect and received only a secretarial acknowledgement. Knowing of the opposition of the Federal Reserve Board to any form and degree of currency expansion, I decided it would be a waste of time to even try to confer with the members of such board. The amendment, with a favorable report from the Banking and Currency Committee, secured an improved status and automatically came before the Senate for consideration and action in regular order.

On April 24, 1933, [Thomas gained the floor] . . . : "Mr. President, for 12 years a policy of deflation, initiated in 1920–21, has been pursued and through that policy we have seen liquidations, we have seen bank failures, we have seen hoarding of money, until today there is not enough money in circulation of all kinds and character, credits, bank deposits and actual currency, [with] which to transact the business of our country. . . .

"The purpose of the amendment is to raise commodity prices. Let me state what will happen under it. I do not say to what extent; I will not be administrator of the power conferred by the amendment. It is possible that nothing might be done under the amendment, but I have a conviction and confidence that something will happen under it.

"The dollar will be cheapened, its buying power will be reduced, and, to the extent that the dollar is brought down in buying power, to the extent that its value is taken out, to that same extent will commodity prices rise. Wheat will go up in value, corn will go up in value, cotton will go up in value, every commodity of the field and the farm and the ranch and the lumberyard and the mine will share in the general prosperity. . . .

"Mr. President, I have tried to state upon this floor hour after hour that we could not make any progress with any matter satisfactorily until we took up and adjusted the money question. That opinion seems to prevail very largely today not only in the United States but throughout the world. I made the statement a moment ago that this deflation, started in 1920 and 1921, has been going on all these years. It hit the farmer first, it hit the stockman second, it hit the small merchant third, it hit the little bank, and then the wholesale houses, and then it hit the factories, then the railroads, and at last it struck all in the Nation. . . .

"Mr. President, what is the condition today? I will not dwell on it at any length. I just want to call attention to one or two facts. A few days ago Mr. William Green of the American Federation of Labor made the statement that we have today 13,000,000 unemployed people in these United States. I hope that is not true, but I am afraid it is. Times have gotten so bad, Mr. President, through unemployment, through the scarcity of money, through the lack of credit, [through] business being at a standstill, that the people cannot get money with which to pay their taxes. Taxes are not being paid because taxes cannot be paid. States, towns, villages, counties, and the Nation itself are having difficulty in getting money to keep themselves going concerns. . . .

"Mr. President, my State is a great agricultural State. In the southern part of my State we produce not much else but cotton. Thirty-five counties in Oklahoma are cotton-producing counties. All landowners and tenants and wage earners in the cities in that section live upon cotton. In the northern half of my State we have a wheat-growing section. The farmers, the tenants, the laborers in the cities live upon wheat. Interspersed in the south and north halves of my State we grow corn. We grow almost everything produced in the North and likewise in the South, so Oklahoma is a great farming State, primarily a farming State. It is true we have oil, we have coal, we have lead and zinc, we have lumber, but in the end those will disappear and the lands alone will remain for future years. When the lead and zinc and coal and oil are gone we will still have our farms, we will still have our farmers and our tenants.

"Let me place in the RECORD at this point what we have been forced to sell our products for in Oklahoma during the past 12 months. Wheat has sold for less than 30 cents per bushel. Corn has sold by the farmer in a range of 8 to 15 cents a bushel. Oats have sold in Oklahoma in a range between 7 and 10 cents a bushel. Cotton sold during the past fall in a range from 5 to 6½ cents a pound. Hogs have sold around $2.75 per hundred, and cattle around $3 per hundred weight.

"Mr. President, in Oklahoma, as in all wheat-growing States, wheat in the past 12 months has been the lowest in recorded history. . . . At this point I want to show the Senate what the farmers of

my State have to produce in order to get money. I have here a pound
of cotton which I exhibit to the Senate. The farmer in Oklahoma,
the farmer in the South, must get land and plough it, plant cotton,
and he and his children and his wife must chop that cotton and
cultivate it. In the fall they must pick it, take it to a gin and have it
processed by being run through a gin, have it baled, and then take
the cotton to the market. This is the size of a bundle, tightly com-
pressed, that he must produce in order to get 5 cents in money. . . .

"I exhibit to the Senate a half-gallon jar containing a very poor
quality of yellow corn shelled. Farmers in Oklahoma and in the
South and East and the West must produce a half-gallon fruit jar
three-quarters full of corn shelled in order to get one-half cent.
That is what the farmers face today. That is what they have faced
during the last 3 years. . . .

"I next show to the Senate another half-gallon jar of wheat. This
is the standard farm commodity of America, grown in my State,
grown in the South, grown in the North, grown in the East, grown in
the West, grown everywhere. Here is a half-gallon jar of wheat. It is a
little more than half full. It contains 2 pounds. The farmers of
America must raise 2 pounds of wheat, plant it, cut it, thresh it, sack
it, haul it to the elevator, to get 1 cent of money. . . .

"In this emergency the States are powerless. Not only are the
States powerless, but the cities and the counties are powerless. They
can do nothing save issue scrip, and that is being done throughout
the length and breadth of the Nation; but the States are protecting their citizens. They cannot get them more money; they cannot
cheapen the dollar; they cannot raise the price of corn, wheat,
cotton, and livestock; but the States almost without exception have
passed laws protecting their citizens. They are protecting those citizens through denying the processes of the courts to those who seek
to foreclose the mortgages existing against the farms and the property of those States. . . . The States themselves are in rebellion
against this policy of deflation; and that act of rebellion is seen in

the passage of innumerable laws throughout the Nation postponing the possibility of foreclosures, repealing laws under which Eastern investors having mortgages on Western properties can secure the process of the courts to enforce those mortgages.

"If that is not rebellion, Mr. President, what is rebellion? The people cannot pay their present indebtedness at these prices. The cities cannot pay. They cannot pay their indebtedness. They cannot pay their interest. They cannot pay their operating expenses. The counties cannot pay. Even the States cannot pay, and the Federal Government itself cannot pay. In the past 3 years the Nation of which we are the policy-making branch has run behind more than $5,000,000,000. We are not collecting enough money, under our existing tax rates, to keep the United States a going concern.

"We raised the tax rate last year, and the higher we raised the rate the larger the deficit. It does not do any good to raise the rates. What good would it do to raise the income tax rate when the people have no incomes? What good would it do to raise the corporation tax rate when the corporations have no net incomes? No good whatever would come from that process. This trouble cannot be solved through that method. . . .

"There is, if my analysis of this depression is right, absolutely no escape from our present imminent danger except through reflation. Nor can we stop to cavil about methods. The situation is too desperate and imperative. The best method is whatever is the quickest. I, too, dislike to load on the President so much responsibility and power, but the alternative is a debate which will delay action, when there is no time to lose. We are at war and must entrust to our Commander in Chief the war-time powers necessary to win this sort of war. The open-market operations, which alone the objectors grudgingly admit might well be used, cannot be entrusted wholly to the Federal Reserve System. They had their opportunity a year ago and made insufficient use of it.

"The Budget cannot be balanced until the people commence

earning money so that they can pay income taxes. The Budget cannot be balanced until corporations again commence earning money, making net earnings, upon which they may be enabled to pay corporate income taxes. They are not doing that now. If deflation persists, the less able will people be to pay the taxes necessary to keep the Government going even upon a reduced annual appropriation Budget.

"Some may wonder why the amendment was prepared in the form it now appears before the Senate and I give the answer. I have been in the Congress for 10 years, in the Senate for more than 6, and I know that we cannot agree upon the silver question; we could not agree upon reducing the gold content of the dollar; we cannot agree upon the exact extent of the expansion of the currency through the buying of bonds. Perhaps we have not the information; perhaps there is some other reason; but it has not been done, and I doubt if it could be done. So the only alternative, if something is to be done, is to confer this power on someone. That someone should be the one who has the confidence of the people of America, someone who is responsible to the people of America, someone who has it in his grasp and power to get the best information, the best expert advice that the Nation and the world afford. This amendment confers that power upon the President, elected by the people by the largest majority ever given a President of this Republic. He has the confidence of the public; he has a record that justifies the bestowal of this confidence; he has the facilities at his command to obtain the best information—in fact all the information—and the best advice, the best brains not only of America but of the world. Because of those facts the amendment confers upon the President a power which we had but which we failed to exercise, and I fear we shall continue to fail to exercise it if this amendment or some similar amendment shall not be enacted. . . .

"As a rule, the bankers are not against this amendment. In my State last year, when I was trying to get more money into circulation

through another means, the banks of my State, apparently not understanding what I was trying to do—and I could not make them
see it, through my inability—were not for my proposal. But times
are so changed in Oklahoma that I do not know of a single bank in
that great State today that is not back of this proposal. The banks
must have it or they will close. . . .

"Mr. President, let us add those figures. The bank resources,
based upon the present value of the dollar, are worth today
$139,000,000,000. United States bonds, based upon the present
buying power of the dollar are worth $51,000,000,000. The bonds
issued by cities, counties, States, and corporations, based upon the
present buying power, are worth, in the products of the sons of toil,
$122,000,000,000. So that in order that the people of the United
States may get rid of their national bonds, their State bonds, their
county bonds, and the other bonds they must produce and sell
products in the sum of $312,000,000,000. The face value is only
$128,000,000,000. There are almost $200,000,000,000 of wealth, of
corn, of wheat, of cotton, of hogs and cattle, [of] human sweat and
toil, which must be produced and expended to pay money to a class
of bondholders who did not earn the money, who did not buy the
money, who do not deserve to keep the money, and that is the
reason why I stated a while ago that this single amendment has
more possible significance than any proposal that has ever come
before the American Congress or any parliament in the history of
the world. If this amendment should be enacted, and if it should be
exercised to the extent of 50 percent, and the dollar cut half in two,
it would transfer that wealth from those who do not own it to the
other side of the ledger, and still the bond-holding class would have
billions they did not buy and did not earn, and the producing class
would not have as many billions as they deserve. . . . "

After general debate of a few days on the amendment, an agreement was reached for a vote which resulted as follows: 64 for, 20
against, 11 absent, and 1 vacancy. The farm bill containing the

amendment was signed by the president on May 12, 1933, and became Public Law No. 10, 73rd Congress, Sec. 821 of Title 31 U.S. Code. Pursuant to the powers conferred by the Congress upon the chief executive to regulate the value of the dollar, President Roosevelt proceeded without delay to take steps to reduce the value of our money. Through public statements the president had made clear his policy and the end sought to be attained — such end being cheaper money and higher prices.

Through a wider use of silver, more dollars were issued into circulation and through a daily increase in the price of gold, the standard gold dollar was gradually reduced in size, hence, weight and value. As the money in circulation was increased, the money unit was diluted, and as the size and weight of the gold dollar was reduced, its value likewise was decreased. The price of the gold ounce was bid up from $20.67 to $35.00 per ounce, which meant that the mint could coin 35 standard gold dollars from one ounce of gold instead of only 20 and 67/100 dollars as provided by the law which had been repealed.

At the time of the revaluation of the gold standard dollar, most bonds and mortgages contained what was known as the gold clause. Such clause provided that payment should be made in "gold coin of the United States of the present standard of weight and fineness." On January 31, 1934, President Roosevelt issued his proclamation reducing the weight of the standard gold dollar from 25.8 grains to 15$\frac{5}{21}$ grains, 9/10 fine, and such smaller gold dollar was by law made legal tender for the payment "of all debts, public and private."

Immediately upon the reduction of the weight of the gold standard dollar by some 40 percent, the holders and owners of gold certificates, gold bonds, and mortgages demanded that they be paid in cither gold dollars of the former weight and fineness or in sufficient currency dollars to equal the value of such former gold dollars. A number of cases involving the validity of the "gold clauses

Thomas broadcasts a speech over NBC at the Century of Progress exhibition in Chicago in 1934. Courtesy Carl Albert Center Congressional Archives, University of Oklahoma.

in obligations" — hence, the constitutionality of the act of May 12, 1933 (Thomas Amendment), the joint resolution of June 5, 1933, and the "Gold Reserve Act of 1934" — were filed and prosecuted in the courts.

Three such cases reached the Supreme Court of the United States on writs of certiorari and were passed upon during the October term, 1934.[50] Mr. Chief Justice Charles Evans Hughes delivered the opinion of the court wherein it was held, in effect, that "gold clauses in obligations" sought to provide two possible plans for payment; [(1) payment in gold as a commodity and (2) payment in legal tender dollars] and that such gold clause obligations, as contained in the instruments before the court, were invalid. The decision upheld the constitutionality of the congressional enactments on the point that the power of the Congress to regulate the currency, under Section 8 of Article I of the Constitution, is superior to the obligation of the bonds. The court decision validated the law whereunder the United States realized a profit of $2.8 billion from the reduction of the weight of the gold standard dollar.

Immediately upon receiving the authority to act as the agent of the Congress in regulating the value of our money, the president began to use such powers to reduce the value or buying power of the dollar. . . . Because of the vast powers granted by the amendment and the clear statement of price policy by the president, prices began to rise, which meant that the dollar began to lose some of its undeserved and, to producers and debtors, ruinous value. From a high value of $1.676 in February 1933, as measured by the Bureau of Labor Statistics, the dollar value fell to $1.41 in December of that same year. The loss of the 26 cents in purchasing power was reflected in higher commodity prices; and the hopes of the author that the deflation might be checked, that reflation might be initiated, that the dollar might be cheapened, and that commodity prices might be increased were already being realized. . . .

At the time the president was authorized to revise our money system, we had less than 500 million silver dollars in our money system. The silver minor coins, such as halves, quarters, and dimes, made up a substantial part of our circulation. When President Roosevelt was inaugurated, silver was denied by law the right to be legal tender for the payment of debts. The amendment provided that all paper notes "and all other coins and currencies heretofore or hereafter coined or issued by or under the authority of the United States shall be legal tender for all debts, public and private."

Since the Congress decided to make a wider use of silver in our money system, we have acquired all the silver that has been offered for sale. When we began to acquire silver, from whatever source, the average price was 25.01 cents per fine ounce. By the year 1945 we had acquired approximately 3,250,000,000 ounces, which at its monetary value of $1.29 per ounce would permit the coining of some 4,192,500,000 silver dollars. While silver is still merely token money, the demand for the metal has so increased as to cause the world price to rise from the 25 cents in 1933 to 90 cents plus per ounce at the present time. . . .

There is no existing authority for coining gold coins of any denomination. The reduction of the weight, hence the value, of the gold dollar and the addition of some $2.5 billion of silver certificates to the circulation, produced the effect contemplated by the new law — such effect being a check to the deflation and a progressive trend of increasing prices. So successful was the monetary adjustment program that by 1937 — a four-year period — prices had been increased to a point where the holders of fixed investments, such as bonds, notes, preferred stocks, and annuities, became vocally alarmed by a fear that our domestic economy was threatened by uncontrolled inflation.

The general public did not know either what had happened or what was taking place, but the members of the Federal Reserve Board, supported by the "money wise bankers," brought forth their favorite scarecrow — inflation — and either intimidated the heads of the government or gave them an excuse to apply the brakes to any further increase in prices. While the general price level had been increased from a low of 64.8 in 1932 to 80.8 in 1936, the dollar still had a value or buying power of $1.238 on the average during the latter year. Such value in terms of commodities and property was almost 25 cents in excess of the value of the dollar during the so-called "Era of Coolidge prosperity."

The Federal Reserve Board and the influential bankers always opposed every effort by the Congress to increase prices so that the people could produce not only to regain their costs but at a profit. After managing our money in such a way as to permit, if not to cause, in the words of T. B. Macaulay[51] of Canada, "by far the most severe depression of which we have any record in history," the members of the board recommended and secured the cooperation of the administration to take immediate and definite steps to check the return of general prosperity. . . . The Federal Reserve Board in its 1937 annual report stated that "in December (1936) the United States Treasury, after consultation with the Board, adopted a policy of placing new gold acquisitions in an inactive account, thus preventing further gold imports from adding to the reserves of member banks."

In August of 1936 the board had raised the reserve requirements for member banks by 50 percent in order to absorb a part of the $3 billion of reserves in excess of requirements held by member banks. The board had already taken action to increase the margin requirements applicable to security loans made by brokers and dealers in securities. All steps taken by the authorities were for the purpose of checking the trend of rising prices. The program to check the rise in prices was successful and brought on the man-made "Panic of 1937."

On page 8 of the board's report for 1937 it was stated that their program had brought a turn in the business situation in the following words: "About the middle of March, prices of stocks and of

lower grade corporate bonds began to decline from the high levels
to which they had risen. Advance buying by industry and trade
slackened, and early in April prices of commodities traded on organized exchanges began to decline." Thus we have a concrete modern example of what can be made to happen by the managers of
money. . . .

At the present time the United States dollar is the "hitching
post" for all the money units of the free nations of the world. . . .
The silver held by the Treasury is valued in terms of gold; otherwise
our government could redeem every dollar of outstanding currency with legal gold and silver dollars. No other nation, in so far as
we know, could make even a respectable start toward redeeming its
outstanding currency in either gold or silver or both at the values
approved by the International Monetary Fund. . . . The United
States is the only nation that has its money unit, the dollar, based
upon a definite and legal gold content; hence, since all the Monetary Fund countries must have their units valued in terms of gold,
the price of such gold having been fixed by United States law at $35
per fine ounce, such nations must have their units valued in dollars
as a prerequisite to dealing in international trade. . . . The United
States dollar — backed by two-thirds of all known monetary gold —
while not redeemable domestically in gold is redeemable in legal
standard silver dollars upon presentation at the Treasury. . . . [S]up-
ported by the strongest, most influential and richest nation[, it] is
without question the best monetary unit in the world.

THE WAR YEARS

In 1939 Senator Royal S. Copeland [D-N.Y.][52] . . . . passed away.
At the time of his death he was chairman of the Subcommittee on
War Department Appropriations, having jurisdiction of items for
the War Department, which embraced appropriations for the Air
Corps. . . . Being the ranking Democrat on the Appropriations

Subcommittee, I succeeded to the position of chairman, made vacant by the death of Senator Copeland.

At that time it had been more than 20 years since the end of World War One, and the public, as well as most members of the Congress, believed that wars were a thing of the past. Acting upon such conviction, and for the want of appropriations, the military department had dwindled until it was almost a memory. The Navy Department was considered our first line of defense, so the Congress was more liberal in its support of that branch of our military program. Support for the War Department, including the Air Corps, reached a low of $251,544,581 in 1924, and during the succeeding ten years the appropriations were kept at almost that annual level.

During the middle and late thirties we knew of the military preparedness program of Germany, Italy, Japan, and a number of the other nations, yet we did not become excited and refused to begin to prepare for a war which we thought would never come to us again. In 1939, the year when war had actually developed in Europe, we spent only $491,298,879 for the support and maintenance of our military establishment.

One of the last efforts of Senator Copeland was to try to secure a modest appropriation to experiment with rubber tires on our French 75-millimeter cannon. Until we entered World War Two the only field pieces of importance we had were guns secured from France after the end of the First World War. The French cannon had wooden wheels and were made to be drawn by horses and mules.

The committee refused to go along with Chairman Copeland, whereupon he took the item to the Senate floor. When the Military Appropriations Bill was being considered by the Senate, the chairman offered an amendment proposing funds for an "educational order" to test the use and efficiency of rubber tires on field cannon. The idea of equipping secondhand cannon with rubber tires, when wars were ancient history, did not appeal to the senators and after a hilarious debate the proposal was practically laughed off the floor.

At that time we had not built a battleship for 20 years. We did not have a single plane equipped with leakless gas tanks, and such planes as we had were equipped with small machine guns and with practically no armor plate protection for the pilots and gunners. The only small arms we had were the Enfield and Springfield single-shot rifles and pistols of various vintages and calibers. At the low stage of our military program, the regular enlisted strength of the army was less than 120,000 men, with some 7,000 officers. When I became chairman of the subcommittee, I realized that we had next to nothing in the way of a fighting military force. For some years the Senate had maintained an investigating committee, and for the lack of something more important to look into, the committee had devoted its time and funds to reporting on and condemning powder and ammunition makers as warmongers.

In October 1939, the German fighting machine under Hitler was already in action. Colonel Charles Lindbergh had visited Europe and upon his return submitted a report advising our people and our government of the extent of the military preparations in a number of the European countries. Still, neither the public nor the administration, including the Congress, evidenced any visible interest in building up our Army, Air Corps, or Navy. Notwithstanding the fact that we did not have either an army or an air force to speak of, and further that the public had lost almost all interest in our military establishment, yet some of us in the Congress could not divest ourselves of the always present responsibility that Section 8 of Article I of the Constitution confers original and exclusive jurisdiction upon the Congress — "To declare war; To raise and support Armies"; and "To provide and maintain a Navy."

Such was the picture confronting me when I assumed the chairmanship of the Senate subcommittee late in the year of 1939. I was not a trained military man. My experience was limited to service in a company of college students; however, our company was not called for service in the war with Spain. In World War One, I registered and waived all exemptions, but obviously due to age I was not called to report for duty. My home city of Lawton is located immediately adjacent to the Fort Sill artillery training center for the Army. When I entered Congress in 1923, I accepted a commission as lieutenant colonel in the Military Intelligence Section of the War Department.

Realizing the importance of the position of chairman of the Senate subcommittee, and at the same time knowing that war had again developed in Europe, I decided to make a survey of our military establishment to ascertain what we had and what we needed in the way of added facilities and equipment to be able to protect our people and our interests in the event the European war should infringe upon and interfere with our citizens, our interests, and our trade. In compliance with what I considered to be my duty, I proposed to the War Department that an immediate investigation be made respecting our military status. I suggested that I would organize a House and Senate group to be made up of members of the . . . appropriations committees of the two branches of the Congress, provided the War Department would furnish the necessary transportation and personnel to accompany and guide the group in making [the] survey.

The trip was arranged and the schedule called for a tour of some 30,000 miles and to require 60 days to complete. Three two-engine planes were made ready for our use. . . . The caravan of planes left Washington in October and visited air fields, army camps, military depots, arsenals, plane factories, and hospitals located in the continental United States, Panama Canal Zone, Hawaii, Alaska, and Puerto Rico.

In flying to the Canal Zone the congressional group was required to land in each country flown over, so brief visits were made to Mexico City, Guatemala City, San Salvador, Managua, Tegucigalpa,

In 1939-1940, Thomas, as chair of the War Department appropriations subcommittee, led a delegation of House and Senate members on an inspection tour of military bases throughout the United States and its territories. Here the delegation quickly discovered that the country was ill-prepared for war. The delegation meets with military officials at Fort Scott, California. From the left are Congressman John M. Costello (D-Calif.); Senator Chan Gurney (R-S.Dak.); Senator Harry S. Truman (D-Mo.); Lieutenant Colonel Edward C. McGuire; Colonel Thomas A. Terry; Senator Thomas; an unidentified officer; Congressman Charles R. Clason (R-Mass.); Senator Sherman Minton (D-Ind.); Congressman John J. Sparkman (D-Ala.); Congressman Thomas E. Martin (R-Iowa); Congressman Charles W. Brooks (R-Ill.); and an unidentified officer. Courtesy Carl Albert Center Congressional Archives, University of Oklahoma.

and San Jose. The more than a dozen military installations in Hawaii were visited by a part of the group and another sub-group visited Alaska, Puerto Rico, and Cuba. No War Department Air Corps installation of substantial size was overlooked. Upon our return we made a report to the Secretary of War, respecting what we found; however, the major part of the report was with reference to personnel and equipment that we did not have.

At El Paso, Texas, we inspected one of our cavalry camps, consisting of some five thousand men and five thousand horses, all well trained for parade purposes. At Fort Knox, Kentucky, we witnessed the initiation of mechanized cavalry, which signaled the fading away of the use of horses in military combat. In our survey we found one anti-aircraft gun at Los Angeles, but no one present knew how to use the weapon. At the same place we found some six-inch cannon mounted on flat cars. At San Francisco we inspected the Coast Guard defenses, but no one present could remember when any of the guns, mounted on the mountain sides, had ever been fired.

We traveled for more than 10,000 miles before we caught up with a Garand rifle. A sample had been exhibited in San Francisco, but the model had been moved on to Fort Riley, Kansas. When we reached the Kansas Cavalry Camp, we saw our first military automatic Garand shooting iron. We saw giant 16-inch cannon hidden away in the jungle of Panama. In Panama we saw equipment somewhat resembling threshing machines, but called sound detectors, but no one could be found to explain just how the clumsy funnels could be used for detecting the approach of hostile aircraft. Such was the condition of the Army and Air Corps when the Congress convened to consider appropriations for the fiscal year beginning July 1, 1941.

The administration sent its budget requests to the Congress, wherein the sum of $853,356,754 was itemized and justified. Notwithstanding the fact that war was in progress in Europe, the House of Representatives reduced the requests to $784,999,094 and the bill, carrying such recommendations, came to the Senate for consideration and action. . . .

The Senate hearings began on April 30, 1940, with General George C. Marshall,[53] chief of staff, and members of the Bureau of the Budget appearing in behalf of the War Department's requests. After the customary preliminary statements, as chairman of the committee, I requested General Marshall to make a clear and definite statement, first, with respect to what the department had in personnel and equipment and, second, what the department needed in order to develop the Army and the Air Force to the point of efficiency considered to be proper in view of the existing war in Europe and the possibility that the United States might become involved in such war.

To my request General Marshall replied as follows: " . . . My own thought is that as the situation grows more critical abroad we ought, step by step — not in a single plunge to repeat those past mistakes in our history where we have gotten indigestion from trying to do everything at once at the last moment — but step by step, to do those things which will put us in a little stronger position . . . so that the military advisors of other governments will recognize our immediate strength and grow cautious accordingly." . . .

During the hearings, Major General H. H. Arnold,[54] chief of Air Corps, made the following statement: "Everything went along beautifully until the Germans went into Poland. Then, it suddenly developed that there were fundamentals, such as leakproof tanks, heavier armament, and the necessity for additional protection for our personnel not incorporated in our planes." The German planes were in three particulars more advanced than our planes. General Arnold advised the committee "that when the German DO-17 was brought down in Scotland, there were 300 bullet holes in it, and 30 bullet holes in the tank. When that airplane hit the ground, the tank still retained its form. Now, with all the metal tanks we have, when the plane hits the ground the tank breaks and the gasoline leaks out; but 48 hours after the crash on the DO-17 in Scotland there were 80 gallons of gasoline in its tanks."

The hearings proceeded from day to day until May 14, 1940, and during such time the committee heard all the recommendations submitted by the representatives of the War Department and all who requested to be heard on special items in the bill. At the conclusion of the hearings on May 14, I made the following statement: "So I think for the time being this completes the hearings. I don't think we should adjourn the hearings until we get a confidential communication from the President, or a confidential communication from the War Department, so I suggest we take a recess subject to call." Such action was taken because the committee was not satisfied with the recommendations which had been made by the representatives of the War Department. The committee had requested a confidential memorandum from the department as to the needs of the Army and Air Force, and such data had not been furnished.

General Marshall had called the chairman of the committee on more than one occasion and advised that the data was being prepared and that just as soon as it was ready he would advise and then such data would be presented at the pleasure of the committee. However, within a few days the chairman was advised that, instead of a confidential memorandum being submitted to the committee, President Roosevelt would ask that a joint session of the House and Senate be convened to the end that he could appear and advise the Congress personally with respect to the enlarged needs of the military establishment.

The president addressed the Congress, outlining the administration's recommendations for a substantial increase in funds with which to speed up the preparedness program. At the conclusion of the president's address to the Congress, the War Department presented its budget request for additional funds for all branches of the military establishment. Upon receipt of the enlarged budget requests, I called my committee together to hear the explanations and reasons for the additional funds. . . .

The president, as commander-in-chief of our military forces, recommended that the Congress restore the cuts made by the House and, in addition, approve the increases contained in the supplemental budget estimates. In the beginning the War Department requested the sum of $853,356,754. The House had approved the sum of $784,999,094. The Senate committee followed the budget and the department's recommendations and reported the bill to the Senate with increases practically doubling the amounts approved by the House. In addition to reporting all items in full, the committee increased the overall amount by the sum of $50,000,000 for the express purpose of carrying the regular Army up to a strength of 280,000. Such was the low status of our Army and Air Force in May 1940. . . .

The House had approved $784,000,000 plus, and the Senate restored the House cuts and then added $712,000,000 plus, so that the bill carried a total of $1,497,711,368 when it was returned to the House of Representatives. The House accepted the Senate increases and thus the preparedness program for World War Two was initiated.

On June 20, 1941, Robert P. Patterson,[55] Undersecretary of War, called at my office in the Senate Office Building and advised, unofficially, that the War Department was in great need of the sum of $500 million to speed up the program for ordnance and chemical warfare plant construction. The detailed plans were for the production of small arms ammunition, smokeless powder, shell-loading plants, TNT, and bag-loading plants.

I asked the undersecretary if he had a budget estimate and he said "No." Then I asked him if the department had surplus funds, not allocated, that could be diverted and used until a regular appropriation could be made. Again the answer was that all funds in the hands of the department were obligated. Then I asked the under-secretary if he had considered securing the needed funds from the R.F.C. [Reconstruction Finance Corporation] and his reply was that it would take too long to convince Jesse Jones,[56] the head of the R.F.C., that the funds were necessary.

Upon being advised that the War Department was in need of funds and that no budget estimate had been secured, it became my duty as chairman of the Senate committee to find a way to either secure the funds or to authorize the department to proceed to make commitments and contracts to construct and equip the nec-essary war production plants. Realizing the need for the war plants and likewise knowing of the predicament in which the department found itself, I immediately outlined a plan to accomplish the end desired.

Under regular departmental procedure an official of whatever rank is not permitted to appear before a congressional committee and request funds . . . without having an approved budget estimate covering the exact item to be secured or constructed. However, it is possible to secure funds from Congress without having a formal estimate, but such cannot be accomplished unless the official mak-ing the request has a friend or friends on the Appropriations Com-mittee. Unbudgeted items may be offered as amendments on the Senate or House floor, but unless such items are of the greatest emergency and of such a character as to permit of public explana-tion, they are almost universally rejected.

With respect to Judge Patterson's request, I advised him that I would call a meeting of my committee at once and that when the committee met I would ask him a number of questions with respect to whether or not his department had ample funds to enable it to proceed with its program of preparedness. While the undersecre-tary, without a budget estimate, could not properly initiate the re-quest for the $500 million, yet if and when a member of the commit-

tee should ask a question about funds necessary to carry forward
the work of the department, it is obvious that an official thus inter-
rogated should make a correct and truthful reply. Oftentimes such
questions and replies are "off the record." Only in cases of "top
secrecy," involving such matters as the development of atomic energy, are officials either justified or excused for not giving full and
complete information with respect to the uses to be made of funds
requested to be appropriated.

On June 20, 1941, my committee met and before the committee
was called to order, I had advised the members relative to the purpose of the meeting. Then, on record, the following proceedings
were had: "Judge Patterson, I have been asking the persons who
have appeared before the committee heretofore, if there were to
be any supplemental estimates to be submitted. I understand that
under the rules and regulations, your Department is not permitted
to ask for money not covered by budget estimates. Last year we had
a similar situation confronting the committee, and at the invitation
of the committee, a year ago, the War Department was requested to
consider the status of our Military Establishment and the status of
the government throughout the world and then to advise the committee within a reasonable time what additional amount of money
should be provided, if any, to speed up our defense machinery. . . . "

Senator Carl Hayden [D-Ariz.]:[57] "I might add, Mr. Chairman,
referring to what happened a year ago, the bill passed the House
of Representatives even under the Budget, and then while we had
it under consideration, the Germans went into Norway, which
aroused our alarm. We called upon the Chief of Staff to state what
he wanted, regardless of the Budget limitations. It took time, of
course, to gather the details. They were to come up here first, as I
remember, on Monday; then that was extended to Friday. On Friday, Hitler went into Holland, and the next Monday the President
submitted to Congress the details that had been worked out by the

General Staff for our purposes. Then when we made inquiry again of the Chief of Staff as to whether everything he would choose was included in the President's submission, he said 'All but 135,000 men,' which item we put in — all done without the Budget estimate. I suggest the same situation obtains here, and that we shouldn't worry about the Budget recommendation or limitation. . . ."

After the opportunity had been granted to the Undersecretary of War to make any request he deemed in the public interest, he proceeded to explain to the committee the need for the $500 million, and because the funds were to be used to build and equip war production plants, most of the testimony was "off the record" which meant that the explanations were not recorded by the official reporters. . . . The record shows that, as chairman of the Senate committee, I was very willing to be liberal in providing funds to develop our program of preparedness. My obvious liberality was due to the knowledge I had received in a two months' tour of investigation of the status of our army and military facilities. Such investigation, on the ground, had disclosed that we had next to nothing in the way of either an army, air force, or military equipment with which to protect our people and our interests covering the entire world.

After the brief session with Judge Patterson the committee, while it could not make any public commitment, unanimously advised the undersecretary that it was convinced that the program outlined was necessary and that the department should proceed to make commitments and contracts on the premise that the necessary funds would be made available at the earliest possible opportunity. Pursuant to the statements made at the hearing and replying upon the advice given by the committee, the War Department proceeded with its program and the $500 million was added to the next bill providing funds for the department under the item "Expediting Production."

LEGISLATIVE HISTORY OF THE ATOMIC BOMB

The authority to make public the legislative history of the atomic bomb was granted to me by Robert P. Patterson, the Secretary of War; also such undertaking was approved by Henry L. Stimson, the former Secretary of War. The fact that the United States was either working upon or had developed a new war weapon known as the atomic bomb did not become known until after the first such bomb was . . . dropped on Hiroshima, Japan. Prior to that time absolutely nothing was known about the atomic energy program save by the president, the Secretary of War, some seven members of the Congress, a very few scientists, and a minimum number of selected civilian and military personnel.

The multiplied thousands engaged in the complex activities connected with the effort no doubt knew that they were employed in war work but they had little, if any, idea relative to the product they were helping to produce. After the world knew that we had secretly developed such a weapon of war, it occurred to me that at least the legislative history of such development should be prepared by some of those who knew about the program during the time when it was the "top secret" of the preparedness effort.

Accordingly, on February 17, 1947, almost two years after the bombs had been used against Japan, I addressed letters to a few officials whom I knew had information respecting the matter. I requested each person addressed to prepare and send to me a statement to the end that a record could be compiled explaining how the program was initiated, how it was financed, and, when completed, the data was to be turned over to the Library of Congress for preservation. The letters mentioned were sent to the following persons: Henry L. Stimson,[58] former Secretary of War; Robert P. Patterson, Secretary of War; Alben W. Barkley [D-Ky.],[59] Senate Majority Leader; Wallace H. White [R-Me.], Senate Minority Leader; and

Styles Bridges [R-N.H.], ranking minority member on the subcommittee having charge of War Department appropriations.

The letters were similar to the one sent to former War Secretary Stimson: "Inasmuch as the development and control of atomic energy has assumed major attention and proportions, it has occurred to me that the legislative history of such development should be prepared and preserved. This legislative history is very brief, but nevertheless it is important. In an effort to develop such history I am sending letters to the members of the small group which assembled in the office of Senator Alben W. Barkley at the time the program for the proposed attempt to develop such energy was first presented to the Senate branch of the Congress and, as we thought, initiated and adopted.

"If you will remember, the meeting referred to was carefully guarded and was highly secretive. No record, and so far as I know, no notes were made of what happened at such meeting. I am sending a copy of this communication to each person who was present at the conference save the persons who attended in the capacity of experts or scientists. I do not have their names and addresses; however, if I can secure same will ask them for a statement also. . . . "

In due time [March 18, 1947] I received a reply from the former secretary as follows: ". . . On my return from a few weeks in South Carolina I have received your letter of February 17th. I quite agree that there should be a brief but accurate record of the legislative aspect of the development of the atomic bomb, and I am glad to send you the following summary of my own recollection of the meeting to which you refer.

"The meeting was held in Senator Barkley's office on June 10, 1944. I had asked Senator Barkley to call such a meeting and, as I recall it, he had selected three other members, who would have leading parts in the appropriation, to be there. These gentlemen were: Senator White, the leader of the Minority on the floor; Senator Thomas of Oklahoma, the chairman of the subcommittee on appropriations relating to military matters; and Senator Bridges of New Hampshire, the senior minority member of that subcommittee. I had with me General George Richards, the Budget Officer for the War Department, and Dr. Vannevar Bush of the Office of Scientific Research and Development. [60] Our purpose in asking for the meeting was to try to make certain that there would be no public discussion of the item in regard to S-1 (the code name for the atomic project) which was in the budget. In the past we had succeeded in saving out of our appropriations for previous years an unused surplus of an amount more than necessary to cover the amounts we were asking in those years. We now felt that we ought not to go further without taking into our confidence the leaders of both houses of Congress so that they would know the purpose of all these appropriations. That was the purpose of the meeting.

"I outlined to them the problem which we faced since I was first asked by the President to be one of the group which handled it. I gave them a sketch of the project and what we were driving at, telling them how the Germans were familiar with such a project of atomic energy before the war and had begun working on it about six months before we had; how by successful bombing of the German installations the Allies had probably put them back so that they were not now ahead of us; but it was a race as to which one would finish first; and that in the successful completion of the research and the construction of the explosive bombs themselves possibly lay the ultimate success of the war.

"The four gentlemen who met us seemed to be very deeply interested. . . . None of them apparently had known anything about it before and they promised that they would help in keeping silent about it and prevent discussion in public as to what it was. Dr. Bush followed what I said and gave more definitely and accurately the scientific nature of the problem in question. The meeting was successful. Under the guidance of the four Senators thus consulted, the necessary appropriations were passed by the Congress and signed by the President.

"I should also like to state as a matter of record my own opinion of the relationship between the executive and the legislative departments in this matter as follows: The passage by the Congress without any public comment whatever of appropriations so vast for a project, whose success no man could surely promise, was a striking demonstration of the courage and daring of the legislative branch of the government. After a single meeting with the responsible officers of the executive branch, leaders both of the House and of the Senate freely pledged their full support, and with confidence in the judgment of these leaders the entire membership of the House and Senate joined in the great adventure by providing the necessary monies without public question or comment. The secret was preserved, the work was continued, and in its final triumph the judgment of the Congress was vindicated."

For almost a quarter of a century the writer was a member of the Senate Committee on Appropriations and from 1939 to 1951, save for two years, was chairman of the subcommittee having charge of funds for the Army, Air Force, and civil functions of the military establishment, and under the Unification Act was chairman of the committee having charge of all appropriations for the military establishment. Due to my position on the committee, it would seem that I should have been able to have known at all times the uses to be made of all funds requested and appropriated. Likewise, it is an assumption that all members of the committees of the two houses knew, or at least had a chance to know, of the reason or reasons behind each budget estimate and request for funds but, fortunately or unfortunately, such was not the case. However, it is obvious that in as much as moneys are appropriated at the beginning of the fiscal year, even the department heads do not know in detail just how all funds made available to them will be expended. The Budget Bureau requires that all funds requested be itemized and justified.

Then the bureau sends its recommendations on the items approved to the president, who in turn forwards the approved estimates to the branches of the Congress.

In times of war the Congress depends upon the administrative branches of the government headed by the president as the commander-in-chief to make the plans, submit the estimates, and carry forward offensively and defensively the program developed and agreed upon. During World War Two the author, as chairman of the Senate subcommittee, held the hearings, reported out the bills and then presented, explained, and defended the items in such bills on the floor of the Senate.

In the early stages of the effort to develop the super-explosive energy, the funds for expenses were taken from appropriations already made for the War Department and the U.S. Army Corps of Engineers. What was done at that time by the war planners obviously was dictated by strategic and security reasons and with both offensive and defensive activities in contemplation. In outlining the program which was developed and followed, there is no intent to criticize either any person involved or step taken, but rather to relate just what happened and then to permit those interested to reach their own conclusions. At all times it should be remembered that our country was at war, and in war, in the opinion of many, the end to be attained justifies the means for accomplishing the results desired.

In making appropriations under the budget system, the law requires that reasons be given for all funds requested and recommended. The items making up the sums appropriated are carried under different and variously designated heads, such as salaries, equipment, clothing, subsistence, transportation, engineer service — army, expediting production, and contingent expenses. The appropriating acts frequently provide for transfer of funds, within specified limits, from one department to another department in the same branch of the government.

Hereunder I set out the amount of funds appropriated for the years 1940–1946 for the War Department, which at the time embraced both the air force and civil function activities:

Fiscal Year	Total Appropriations Including Deficiencies	Amount of Carry Over
1940	851,549,995	None
1941	8,480,594,407	None
1942	75,462,593,587	1,317,103,538
1943	42,820,006,365	32,368,908,636
1944	59,034,839,673	15,176,410,288
1945	15,434,814,795	32,766,013,604
1946	21,496,902,030	10,397,270,501

From the foregoing vast sums made available to the War Department, which as stated included the Air Force and the engineers, the money necessary to start and carry forward the atomic energy project was taken. Due to the large sums carried over, it was not difficult to secure the necessary funds for the purpose mentioned. When the possibility of developing the super-explosive was first suggested and considered by the war managers, no member of either the House or Senate, in so far as I can learn, was let in on the secret.

When we now reflect upon the development of the war program and realize that almost every important step was ferreted out by the keen newspaper fraternity, it is [understandable] that those in authority guarded the atomic bomb development with the utmost secrecy. At that time (June 1942) due to the fact that Army camps, airfields, manufacturing plants, and military establishments of every kind were being located, constructed, and operated with more or less secrecy, it was not difficult for the authorities to secure vast tracts of land; remove the inhabitants; construct roads, buildings, utilities, and housing; and then equip such buildings with machinery and begin and continue operations on the broad and all inclusive explanation that such facilities were war plants. At that time many of the war projects were classified — meaning secret.

On one occasion in my own state of Oklahoma, I visited the various areas where war facilities had been constructed. As a rule, on such trips, I would be accompanied by small delegations of local citizens who were appreciative of the fact that they had an important war plant located in their area. When I visited the Burns Flat air facility located between Clinton and Elk City, I found a vast tract equipped with the usual kind and number of buildings and a large area set aside for the use of aircraft. In Oklahoma the air runways had been constructed of many and various kinds of materials and some of the air strips were not holding up satisfactorily under the traffic imposed thereon. While I had no complaint from Burns Flat, yet I was anxious to see the runways. I remember making inquiries about the airfield, the materials in the runways, the kind, size, and number of aircraft in use — all the time expecting to be driven to the field where I could see for myself the items of interest. However, after having spent considerable time in the canteen, soft drink bar, the library of few books, quarters for the personnel, and the mess hall, it eventually dawned upon me that the commanding officer did not intend to let me even see the area containing the planes and the operating field. When away from the facility I learned that no persons in the adjacent area had any idea of the kind of training activities that were being carried on in their immediate vicinity.

On another occasion in the Senate Committee on Appropriations chamber, Senator Kenneth McKellar [D-Tenn.],[61] then acting chairman, disclosed that he had something in his state of Tennessee which he feared might turn out to be a "white elephant." He stated that the government had secured a very large tract [and] had constructed many buildings and a vast number of residences; that the land was being enclosed with an expensive form of fencing, and that no one, not even the contractors constructing the improvements, had any idea as to what use was to be made of the project.

Such statements at that time caused no unusual comment, as most of the committee members had projects in their own states that were either classified or were never used. Later the classified Tennessee development became known as the Manhattan Project for the production of atomic energy.

In order to further show the extreme secrecy surrounding the atom bomb development, in June 1943, one year after the effort was initiated, Senator Harry Truman [D-Mo.], chairman of the Special Committee to Investigate the National Defense Program, requested Secretary Stimson to assist his committee in arranging for holding "a meeting in the neighborhood of Pasco, Washington, to investigate conditions at the Hanford Engineer Works." At the insistence of the Secretary of War, the "legislative investigation" was "held in abeyance until the project had served its war purpose or until the then existing security restrictions could be lifted."

Still later, in 1944, Senator [Monrad] Wallgren [D-Wash.] . . . requested and insisted that the Senate committee proceed to "investigate complaints regarding the housing at Pasco." Again the Secretary of War refused to grant the request. Whereupon the chairman, Senator Truman, proposed "that Brigadier General Frank Lowe[62] and Lieutenant Colonel Harry Vaughn[63] be sent by the Committee to Pasco solely for the purpose of investigating questions of waste with respect to constructing of housing, roads, and other matters not relating to the processes of manufacture, or other secrets, connected with the Manhattan Project."

Being denied the opportunity for investigating the secret work being carried on at Hanford, "the Chairman of the Committee," Senator Truman, "indicated his firm conviction that the proposed arrangement was such as to preclude any assumption that General Lowe could not safely be permitted to examine into the non-secret portions of the project in the vicinity of Pasco." Again the request involving even an inspection of the non-secret activities adjacent to the Washington state atomic energy installation was denied.

Secretary Stimson explained that he declined "to take into his confidence any further persons, whether they be army officers or civilians" and "that he — Secretary Stimson — would have to accept the responsibility for any waste or improper action which might otherwise be avoided by the normal functioning of the committee." Thus ended the requests of the Truman committee to make "investigations on the ground in the vicinity of the plants." From the very beginning, everything connected with the effort to develop the atomic bomb was not only labeled but positively treated with "top secrecy."

Late in 1943 another effort was made by Congressman Albert Engel [R-Mich.] . . . to secure information "concerning the Manhattan project construction taking place at Oak Ridge, Tennessee." Congressman Engel was a conscientious, hard-working member of the House Subcommittee on War Department Appropriations. On his own motion and at his own expense he made frequent trips to inspect military facilities in order that he might acquaint himself with respect to the need for funds to support such projects. Congressman Engel advised the Undersecretary of War that he had requests for information respecting the Oak Ridge installation and that he "stated his intention of visiting the plant site in the near future." According to my report, "Mr. Engel was informed by the Undersecretary of War concerning the highly secret status of the project and that the information requested by him could not be supplied at that time." Like Senator Truman, Congressman Engel "was also prevailed upon to refrain from making his contemplated visit to the plant site."

During the first years of the war no budget estimates or requests, for obvious reasons, were submitted to either the House or the Senate for funds to be used for even research work in connection with the development of atomic energy. In so far as I can learn, neither the members of the Truman investigating committee nor Congressman Engel ever received or secured any information whatever re-

specting the attempted development of the super-explosive atomic
energy. To this date I know of only seven members of the Congress
who even suspected that an atomic bomb was in the making. The
seven members were as follows: Sam Rayburn [D-Tex.], Speaker of
the House of Representatives; John W. McCormack [D-Mass.],[64]
Majority Leader in the House; Joseph W. Martin [R-Mass.],[65] Minority Leader in the House; Alben W. Barkley [D-Ky.], Majority leader
in the Senate; Wallace White, Minority Leader in the Senate; Styles
Bridges,[66] ranking minority member on the Senate subcommittee
having charge of War Department appropriations; and myself, the
chairman of the said Senate subcommittee having charge of War
Department appropriations.

Not having been present when the group of three House members were advised of the effort and program to develop the super-
power of energy, I cannot relate either the nature of the conference
or the degree of information given the congressmen. In so far as I
can learn, no member of the House Committee on Appropriations,
save Congressman Engel, was advised or knew that war plants were
in existence at either Oak Ridge, Tennessee, or Pasco, Washington.
My first and only information came about as follows:

In the early morning of June 10, 1944, Senator Barkley called me
over the telephone and asked me to come to his office, giving the
particular room number, at 10:30 A.M. that day. He asked that I not
advise any person of my whereabouts as there was to be an important conference that should not be disturbed. He also suggested
that I should come unattended.

At the appointed time I appeared at the mentioned room and
found others already there. One by one the senators and others
invited made their appearance. When all had arrived the conference was made up of the following: Secretary of War Stimson; Major General Richards, representing the war budget department;
Dr. Vannevar Bush, an eminent scientist; Senators Barkley, White,
Bridges, and myself. When all had assembled Senator Barkley ad-

vised his colleagues that he had called the conference at the request of Mr. Stimson, Secretary of War, and then asked the secretary to state the reason for the call and conference.

Secretary Stimson began by apologizing for the unavoidable absence of General George C. Marshall. He then stated the importance of the conference and that everything to be said would be relative to the war effort and in the strictest confidence. After securing satisfactory evidence that the proceedings were to be considered and treated as "top secret," the secretary proceeded to inform the senators of the presence in the pending War Department Appropriation Bill of an item covering work on atomic fission for the next — 1945 — fiscal year. To that moment the matter of "atomic fission" had never been mentioned in my presence. When first suggested, I did not know what the words meant, and now some seven years later I am still almost wholly in the dark with respect to both the development and content of the atomic bomb.

In order that I may not make a misstatement with respect to that meeting, I will quote from a report prepared at my request and first marked "Secret," then later the secrecy was removed, as follows: "He ('Secretary of War Stimson') referred to the importance of this work becoming evident in 1939 with the scientific discovery of the theoretical possibility of making an explosive of enormous power by this atomic fission method. He traced the efforts made since that time, referring to the necessity of constructing extensive manufacturing facilities in order to obtain the desired results, and mentioned that this fact made it possible for a rich nation only to pursue such development. An indication of the effect of the final product was given by stating its equivalent in tons of TNT and the extent of devastation that could be thus produced. The time schedule was approximated only by stating that the appropriations bill item contemplated the completion of construction and operation during the coming fiscal year. He gave the approximate physical size of the bomb and indicated that it could be carried by a single aircraft."

As I now remember, it was stated in the conference that a relatively small amount of the product—not described—could be carried in a single aircraft and when dropped on a city or area would, when exploded, do as much damage as 10,000 tons of any explosive known of at that time. The secretary stated further that "in case of a deadlock this single new development might determine the outcome of the war." Dr. Bush—still quoting from the original secret report—"presented a somewhat more scientific status of the matter and said that there was then no scientist either in Britain or the United States associated with this matter who did not believe that the program would be successful." The secret report stated in parenthesis: "(The reference to universal belief of the British and American scientists is believed to have been somewhat exaggerated)."

The secretary made the statement that in the event the German government was able to develop the energy first, the war would soon be over for the reason that no nation could stand the impact of such terrific force. Then he followed through by stating that in the event we could develop the energy and perfect it first, the war would likewise be over for the same reason that neither the German nor the Japanese governments could exist with such power being used against them.

While speaking only for myself, I secured the very definite impression that the undertaking—the effort to develop atomic energy—was of recent origin—in fact only in the preliminary or research stage. As I now remember, there was nothing said or even intimated that the project was already well under way and that prior to that date upwards of $2 billion had already been expended in the various phases of the effort to develop atomic energy.

After we had been advised that the nation first perfecting the powerful energy would be able to terminate the war at once and that the scientists were of the opinion that we could succeed in producing such energy, as one of the group, I was convinced that we should proceed with all possible speed to develop and use the all powerful war weapon. An inquiry as to the cost brought the answer, as I understood, that the War Department wanted $800 million with which to begin the undertaking. The writer, as chairman of the Senate committee, having presented and secured the passage of a single bill through the Senate carrying some $72 billion for the War Department, and knowing that there was a carry-over of some $32 billion from the 1942 and 1943 appropriations, I was confident that the securing of the funds for the purposes mentioned would not present a difficult problem.

I had long before learned that the larger and more complicated the legislative bill the easier it was to secure favorable action on the Senate floor. Short simple bills or bills proposing small appropriations sometimes call for long debate. Such measures the members can readily understand and among ninety-six senators there are always a sizeable number who are ready to make a speech on any question they can master without too much effort. A bill containing a few hundred pages of definitions and explanatory matters, or a measure proposing to appropriate seventy-odd billions of dollars is too large to tackle without special preparation. As a rule, the larger the appropriation bill in war times the quicker it can be passed; hence, the $2 billion used to develop the bombs dropped on Japan, and the billions appropriated and used since that time, have occasioned little debate in the Senate.

In the early days of World War Two there was no definite and specific authority for appropriating money to develop such energy, and because of the necessary secrecy connected with and surrounding the endeavor, it would not have been in the public interest at that time to have suggested legislation proposing such authority. Therefore, because of the existence of the war and the secrecy with which the effort was surrounded, the original money expended to develop the atomic bomb was taken from funds already appropriated for such purposes as "Engineer Service — Army" and "Expediting Production."

In order to make this record, I will enumerate hereunder the total amount of funds used for the Manhattan Project during each fiscal year up to and including 1946, when the first Resolution — Senate Bill 1717 — was introduced, passed and approved on August 1, 1946, and became Public Law 585,79th Congress,2nd Session, and known as the "Atomic Energy Act of 1946."

The amount of funds allocated to the Manhattan Project and secured from money appropriated to the War Department was:

Fiscal Year	Amount
1943	385,001,112.00
1944	422,933,396.70
1945	1,069,929,509.74
1946	567,658,130.60
1947 (to 12/31/46)	134,976,911.35
Total	2,580,499,060.39

The amount of expenditures including advancement of funds by the Manhattan District to other organizations during each fiscal year was:

Fiscal Year	Amount
1943	77,098,355.73
1944	729,981,724.61
1945	856,901,959.02
1946	356,056,772.82
1947 (to 12/31/46)	171,419,990.82
Total	2,191,458,803.00

The amount of funds advanced to other government agencies for certain phases of the work performed under the Manhattan District for each of the years was as follows:

Fiscal Year	Amount
1943	
1944	300,000.00
1945	2,000,000.00
1946	374,000.00
1947 (to 12/31/46)	8,835,500.00
Total	11,509,500.00

The customary annual budget procedure was not followed during the early period of the project. Funds required were received from time to time through allotments from funds available to the War Department. The first budget request for funds to produce atomic energy was transmitted to the Office of the Chief of Engineers on February 3, 1945, for the fiscal year 1946. . . .

The secretaries of the congressional committees and their assistants are among the most competent and efficient officials of the government. The secretaries to the more important committees are developed through long years of service and are regarded as career officers of the respective houses of the Congress. To my request for information I received the following: "At no time during the consideration of appropriations dealing with the prosecution of the war, either on the record or off the record, was the atomic bomb ever mentioned. The first direct reference to it appears in the hearings on the Military Establishment Appropriation Bill, 1947, before the War Department Subcommittee of the House Appropriations Committee. . . . During the war years, we had no knowledge in the committee as to what appropriations were available and used for this purpose."

FUNDS USED FOR THE MANHATTAN PROJECT

For the first time in any hearing, the funds used for the construction of the Manhattan Project were discussed in the House hearings on the Military Establishment Appropriation Bill for 1947, at which time the project was set up as an independent appropriation item for Atomic Service in the amount of $375 million. In May 1946, before the House Appropriations Committee, General Thomas Handy,[67] General Leslie Groves,[68] and General Richards referred to the funds by which the Manhattan Project was developed. . . . During the war, funds for the Manhattan Project were mixed in with other funds, including Engineer Service for the Army, and made available to the Chief of Engineers for construction — the funds being hidden then for a purpose under the cover of the War Department.

General Groves stated: "I would like to put on the record a statement of my personal appreciation for the support that I got from the Congress, and particularly from this subcommittee of the Committee on Appropriations, in permitting this work we were engaged to go ahead, taking the chances that each member of this committee took with his future political career on the very scanty information that we had to give you at that time. You took desperate chances, just as we took desperate chances, I think, with the reputation of all the members of the subcommittee involved in it, all of the members of the Committee on Appropriations who knew about it, took the same chances as I did. I was staking my military reputation on the success of the project, just as each one of you was staking your political reputation. . . ."

On September 8, 1945, the Senate Special Investigating Committee, acting through its Chief Counsel, made application for permission to investigate the said Clinton Engineering Works, located at or near Pasco, Washington. Again, the War Department advised that its position with respect to secrecy of the Manhattan Project had not changed, whereupon the Committee did not insist upon making the investigation.

In August, 1945, combat use of atomic bombs had been made and thereafter the Senate Committee was advised that its members might visit the Hanford Engineer Works.[69] The Committee submit-

ted a list of the items it wanted to look into — such list including
costs of entire project with a breakdown of the detailed cost of each
installation thereof, scale of wages paid, and labor turnover.

On August 20, 1945, upon arrival of the delegation at Pasco
Naval Base, of some fourteen members and consisting of Senators,
counsel to the Committee, special investigators, secretaries, Gen-
erals, Colonels and other persons, they were taken to the officers'
mess for luncheon. After luncheon the delegation was taken to
Richland for briefing at Colonel Norman Matthias's office and the
reasons explained for the enormous reservation which the project
occupies. The briefing included a discussion of costs and other
matters having no connection with the purpose of the installation.

After the briefing, the Committee was then informed that they
would be taken into two manufacturing buildings which at the present time were highly restricted. They could ask no questions as
to . . . the processes involved. As representatives of their Government, it was expected that they would safeguard and refrain from
discussing anything which they saw in any of the buildings. They
were then taken to the hospital where each individual submitted to
a blood test before proceeding to the manufacturing areas.

At this point, the party was divided into groups of 3 each and
placed in cars, each of which was driven by an officer. . . . On the way
to the manufacturing areas, the various types of housing erected in
Richland Village were pointed out, with the statement that all housing was erected under lump sum contract and that they were within
the statutory limitations as to cost. The group was advised that the
occupants of the houses were held responsible to keep the premises
in a neat and presentable condition, and that they had done their
own seeding, with government-furnished seed. The Senators were
informed of the number of miles of road constructed, railroads,
and other pertinent information.

The group was driven through the old Hanford Camp to impress
them with the fact that only the barest minimum was constructed.

From the Hanford Camp the group proceeded to the 100-F Area where they were shown through the experimentation being conducted . . . on salmon and steelhead trout, the two most important fish in the Columbia River.

They were next shown through the main pump house, filtration plant, and water cooling plant. In the pile building they were shown the face of the pile and the control room. From there the party proceeded to the other pile areas, but did not enter. The purpose of this was to impress upon the Senators the necessity for the long distances between manufacturing areas, and they were informed that it was for safety precautions only.

In the 200-F Area, . . . the three Senators, donning protective clothing . . . were taken to the upper floor to be shown the remote control procedures employed in operating this building and were permitted to view them through the periscopes on the cranes in use. The party then proceeded to the MP mess hall, where they were served supper, prior to returning them to the Naval Base at Pasco, where they took off for Spokane that evening.

The committee "was informed that they were the first civilians who were not directly connected with the project that had ever been permitted to enter the buildings." . . . From the foregoing record, it is not difficult to understand why the members of the Congress, as well as the public, were kept in the dark with respect to the development of the atomic bomb. . . .

CONGRESSIONAL JUNKETS

In recent years some of our magazines and news sheets, as well as some of our people, have criticized, if not condemned, the Congress for appointing committees to make investigations relative to matters affecting the public interest. . . . Because of the status of the United States among the world powers, because our people have interests in all other countries, and because our taxpayers are being called upon to raise vast sums to be expended abroad, the Congress, the policy-making branch of the government, has adopted a policy of securing all available information and data respecting the need for and the advisability of cooperating with the other nations for security, peace, and prosperity. . . .

Some editors, columnists, and cartoonists have referred to the committee investigation trips abroad as "congressional junkets." According to some interpretations, a congressional junket is defined as "an outing at public expense." Having participated in a number of congressional committee trips abroad, I am familiar with the purposes of such trips, and likewise with the expenses or costs to the government. In 1927 and again in 1928 I was a delegate to the Inter-Parliamentary Union meetings—one held at Paris and the other at Berlin. To such meetings the government contributed for expenses the sum of $500 to each delegate.

In 1936 the Senate Committee on Indian Affairs appointed a subcommittee of three members to visit Alaska to learn, firsthand, about the area known as "Uncle Sam's Attic." At that time the Indians and Eskimos were in distress; a farm colonization scheme was being promoted, and war bases were being suggested. The trip from Washington to Seattle was by rail; from Seattle to Alaska and return was by Coast Guard cutter; and then back to Washington by rail—all at a total cost to the government of less than $1,500.

At that time, round trip tickets to the west coast were on an excursion rate basis, and charges on the U.S. Coast Guard ship plying Alaskan waters were $1.50 per day. The information secured was made available to the Committees on Indian Affairs, Agriculture, and Appropriations. On a single item, the data secured saved the government over $1 million in the amount paid to a private company for their claim to ownership of Alaskan reindeer.

The 1939 trip of inspection of Army and Air Force camps, bases, depots, arsenals, and manufacturing plants gave the committee information respecting our unpreparedness for war and resulted in forcing the two branches to begin a preparedness program in the early summer of 1940. When the foot and mouth disease broke out among the cattle in Mexico, I accompanied a committee to that country in an effort to find out what might be done to keep the disease away from the United States. It may be noted that to date the "Aftosa Malady" has not reached the divided hoofed animals of our country.

In 1945, as a representative of the Senate Committee on Agriculture and Forestry, I was a delegate to the Food and Agriculture Organization held at Quebec. Again, in 1946, I attended the second meeting of the F.A.O. held at Copenhagen, and likewise in 1947 I attended the third meeting held in Geneva. The United States representatives to such conferences were reimbursed for their necessary expenses. Our publicly owned and operated airplanes and steam ships were used for transportation purposes.

In addition to attending the F.A.O. meeting at Copenhagen, Denmark, I visited Germany to look into the reasons for the heavy expenditures being made for occupation and rehabilitation purposes. Upon my return I made a report to the War Department respecting the progress being made and in such report I gave an account of the final days of the trial of the high German command convicted at Nürnberg of being responsible for the atrocities committed during World War Two.

NÜRNBERG

The trial, being the first of its kind ever held, and the prisoners being confronted by a jury representing four nations, and being accused under so-called international laws prepared and promulgated after the acts had been committed, was so unique that I included my observations of such proceedings in my report to the Congress and to the heads of the administrative branches of the government. That portion of my report relating to the trial was as follows: . . . Nürnberg, the place of the trial, is located in the American zone; hence, our khaki-clad soldiers were on duty and in evidence in all parts of the city and in the surrounding country.[70]

Nürnberg was selected for the place of trial for the following reasons: The city, formerly containing half a million inhabitants, was chosen by Hitler as Nazism's cultural center. The city was the capital of the Nazi Party Congress. While the city was some 75 percent destroyed, the court house called the Palace of Justice was not greatly damaged. Immediately adjacent to the court house is a modern jail with cells for four hundred prisoners. Hence, Nürnberg was a natural for the most celebrated trial of all history.

At Paris I took off late in the afternoon to attend the final session of the trial. There were no lighting facilities at the airport in Nürnberg, so I had to land at Frankfort and drive the almost 200 miles in order to attend the last sessions of the International Military Tribunal. After an all night drive I arrived at Nürnberg at 5 o'clock in the morning. Our three-star automobile, the property of General Lucius Clay,[71] was stopped and inspected at almost every turn. The members of my party had special cards of identification, but the American military authorities were taking no chances of permitting unauthorized persons reaching the closing sessions of the world-famous trial.

Here is the picture of the last day of the famous trial as I saw it. The court room was about the same size and resembled the court rooms in our local court houses. On the last day the court convened at 9 o'clock A.M. The prisoners, pale and emaciated and in various forms of dress, were in the dock surrounded by the smartly clad soldiers of the United States.

The soldiers at every door were giants in size and were ready for any emergency. Their suits of army woolens were perfectly tailored and fit like gloves. They wore steel helmets, enameled white. Broad white web belts encircled their waists. Each wore white gloves and carried a sturdy police club also enameled white. To complete their glamorous outfit, each wore red cords around his shoulders, and their black shoes were topped with white leggings or spats.

The soldiers of no other country could present a comparable picture. Only a few military uniforms were worn by the German prisoners. Hermann Goering, the first deputy under Hitler and Number One Nazi leader, was dressed in conventional grey, but the suit had been made when he was a much heavier man. Now he was only a shadow of his former self.

Presently the judges, in flowing black gowns, solemnly filed in and took their seats at the elevated table. The attorneys for the prosecution as well as for the defense occupied seats at the elevated table. The attorneys for the prosecution, as well as for the defense, occupied the space between the four-nation court, on the one side, and the dejected war prisoners on the other. Behind the judges stood the standards containing the victorious flags of Russia, Great Britain, France, and the United States. The presiding judge was Lord Chief Justice Sir Geoffrey Lawrence of Britain.

When the court was called to order every seat on the floor and in the galleries was occupied. Each seat in the room was numbered and each had attached thereto a headphone set. The court, the prisoners, the attorneys, and the spectators all had their headphone sets in place. The proceedings were conducted in Russian, French, English, and German.

The judges took turns in reviewing the charges and the evidence against the prisoners. It made no difference what language was used — the interpretation was instantaneous into the language understood by the listener; hence, there was no delay for interpretations. Each one of the prisoners heard a summary of the evidence against him and the verdict of the court as to his guilt or innocence.

The prisoners were indicted on four counts. Each prisoner was charged with having conspired to commit crimes against the peace by planning, preparing, and initiating a war of aggression. They were charged with war crimes by violating the laws, treaties, and

customs of war. They were charged with crimes against humanity—
namely, enslavement, extermination, and murder. It took eighty
thousand words to catalogue the crimes charged in the indict-
ments, and it required a day and a half for the court to present the
reviews, summaries, and findings.

During one session of the court, and while the prisoners were in
the dock, I was shown through the prison. My guide was the prison
superintendent, Colonel Selby Little, formerly of Fort Sill, Oklahoma, and who had married a girl from my home city of Lawton. I
visited every cell occupied by the once proud and haughty German
leaders.

Each had a small individual solid concrete room. The cells were
small—save the ceilings were high. On one wall there was a small
opening for light and ventilation. The opening was protected by
heavy iron bars. Instead of glass the light came through a clear
plastic, something that will not break and afford a sharp cutting
edge. Each cell contained a heavy iron cot, a long used mattress,
and two blankets. A small flimsy table was provided. One plain
wooden chair and a specially devised open toilet made up the fur-
nishings. All hooks, nails, and electronic wires had been removed.
There was nothing available that could be used in a suicide attempt.

The mess provided consisted of porridge—a kind of hash—
three slices of dark bread, and coffee. No metal knife or fork or
spoon was provided. A frail wooden spoon was permitted. When the
meal was over all vessels were removed. At night the reading glasses
and spectacles were removed from each cell. In the door was an
opening just large enough to permit of the passing in of food,
books, and articles of clothing. The opening was heavily barred and
was kept locked from the outside. Night and day—during every
hour and every minute—a strong, alert American soldier stood
before the door of each cell and constantly observed the move-
ments of his prisoner. Near the row of cells containing the twenty-
one prisoners was a small chapel and such as requested were per-

mitted to attend the services provided. Such was the life they lived
during the ten months of the trial. How different from the scenes of
pomp and splendor which they enjoyed prior to the fall of their
projected empire.

In my tour of the prison I entered the dingy cell of Goering, the
Number One German war prisoner. . . . Goering was Hitler's Crown
Prince — the great Reichsmarshal. Chief of the Luftwaffe, President
of the Reichstag, architect of the Gestapo, dictator of German economy, the man who ordered Allied airmen in prison war cages mur-
dered, and the man of whom the high court said, "His guilt is
unique in its enormity."

The noon hour was over and the sentencing of the prisoners was
set for 3 o'clock P.M. Again the court room was filled. Only those
having special permits were in their seats. The dock was vacant. The
chairs had been removed. Immediately behind the dock was a narrow sliding door — just wide enough for one person at a time to
enter or retire.

Promptly at the appointed hour the High Court Marshal cried
out: "Attention! Attention! Take your seats!" The judges, again in
somber black, entered and the court sat. Such was the picture when
the sentences were pronounced. Amid a deathly silence the sliding door, operated by electricity, clicked and moved aside, and
one after the other, two strong American military police, dressed
for the occasion, quickly stepped inside the room and took their
places, one on each side of the door. They were quickly followed by
Goering — Prisoner Number One, and he was followed by a third
strong American M.P. A headphone set was handed the prisoner
and he made his own adjustments. Without delay Lord Chief Justice Lawrence, in measured words, pronounced the sentence as
follows: "HERMANN WILHELM GOERING, ON THE COUNTS
ON WHICH YOU HAVE BEEN FOUND GUILTY, THE INTERNA-
TIONAL MILITARY TRIBUNAL SENTENCES YOU TO DEATH
BY HANGING." For a brief moment the condemned prisoner

gazed at the judges. Then, realizing that this was all, he whisked off his headgear, wheeled quickly about, returned through the narrow sliding door, and disappeared forever.

It took about a minute and a half to return the first condemned man to his cell and to produce in court the second—Joachim von Ribbentrop. Then followed the same procedure and the same sentence. One by one the prisoners were produced, sentenced, and returned to their solitary cells to await the execution. On Wednesday, October 16th, in the high-walled prison yard adjacent to the Palace of Justice, the sentences were carried out. Nine of the war prisoners were hanged—not executed honorably as soldiers die, but disgracefully, like common criminals. Goering, the tenth, too cowardly to face the gallows, deserted his comrades in crime and committed suicide a few minutes before he was to be hanged. This kind of a trial will never again be necessary.

TRIP TO INVESTIGATE EXPENDITURE OF MARSHALL PLAN APPROPRIATIONS

After the Congress adjourned in 1949, the Senate Committee on Appropriations appointed a subcommittee to investigate how the funds advanced to the Marshall Plan countries in Europe were being used. Due to the fact that I was chairman of the Subcommittee on Military Appropriations, I was selected to head the committee. The members of the committee used military planes and army transports to cross the ocean to Europe. The several senators assembled at Paris and started on their mission on October 22, 1949.

A plane was assigned to us by the Air Force. From Paris we flew to Brussels, Belgium. From there we flew to The Hague, in the Netherlands; from The Hague, we flew to Oslo, Norway; from Norway we flew to Stockholm, Sweden. From Stockholm we flew back south to Copenhagen, Denmark; from Copenhagen, we flew to Frankfort, Germany; from Frankfort we went to Heidelberg and other cities in

In October 1949, members of the U.S. Senate Subcommittee on Military Appropriations visit Luxembourg while on a fact-finding mission to determine how funds were being spent in countries receiving Marshall Plan money. From the left are A. Willis Robertson (D-Va.); John C. McClellan (D-Ark.); Perle Mesta, U.S. minister to Luxembourg; an unidentified speaker; Elmer Thomas; Dennis Chavez (D-N.Mex.); and Burnet R. Maybank (D-S.C.). Courtesy Carl Albert Center Congressional Archives, University of Oklahoma.

the western zone of Germany. We also went to Berlin. From Berlin we flew to Luxembourg; from Luxembourg we flew to Geneva, Switzerland, and from Geneva we flew to Vienna, Austria; from Vienna we flew to Athens, Greece; from Athens we flew to Rome; from Rome we flew across to Madrid, Spain; from Madrid we flew to Paris. From Paris we flew to London, and from London we embarked upon our various means of transportation back to the United States. . . .

Upon our return to Washington, I made a report to Senator McKellar, chairman of the Senate Committee on Appropriations, and in addition, copies of the report were sent to the president and to the heads of each department of the government. . . . "Of the total appropriations made, some seven billion dollars were for aid and assistance to countries and peoples located and residing in the Eastern Hemisphere. It was because of the vast appropriations made and the additional requests for money to be expended outside the United States that my committee made the trip to Europe. A break-down of the foreign-aid funds is as follows: The sum of over $4,700,000,000 was appropriated to aid and assist the Marshall Plan countries. The sum of over $900,000,000 was appropriated for civil government and rehabilitation of peoples in the occupied areas of Europe. The sum of over $1,300,000,000 was appropriated to organize, equip, and arm troops in the countries which are members of the Atlantic Pact. The sum of $45,000,000 was appropriated for aid and assistance to Greece and Turkey. And the sum of $76,000,000 was appropriated for aid and assistance to Palestine refugees and to Korea. These vast appropriations were recommended by the administration and, without respect to political parties, were voted by the Congress.

"Why were such appropriations made? The reason and basis for such vast expenditures is fear of war with Russia. At this time the peoples of the world are dividing into two groups. One group known as Communists are being organized by Russia, and the other group composed of free peoples who want to be and remain free, are being organized and assisted by our own United States.

"World War No. 1 placed our country among the few great nations of the earth, and World War No. 2 forced upon us the leadership of the free peoples of the world. Without either planning or striving, destiny has placed world leadership in our hands. No nation, other than our own, is able either economically or financially, to organize, equip, and lead the peoples who want to be and remain free in this titanic struggle to check the spread of communism throughout the world. In this dark hour of the world's history, our own country—the richest, the strongest, and the most influential of all—cannot escape its responsibilities. Should we fail, or even hesitate, Russia stands ready to take over. The fall of free governments and free people into the communistic state is too horrible to contemplate. . . .

"It was because of this ever-present communistic threat and fear that the recent Congress appropriated such vast sums to try to check and stop the spread of this ungodly economic and political way of life. The Congress believes that it is better to try to prevent another world-wide war than to await the development of hostilities and then be forced to prepare for and wage another terrible contest. . . . It was to prevent such a possible calamity that the Congress made such lavish appropriations. . . .

"To reach Europe, Senator Edward Thye [R-Minn.] and I flew the Atlantic. The other Senators went across on an Army transport. After reaching Europe our Military Establishment furnished us a plane equipped with regular military personnel. The Air Force pilots and crew members are required to spend a certain amount of time in the air as a part of their regular training program; hence, we secured our transportation at no additional cost to the Government.

"Our committee visited countries receiving Marshall Plan aid. Also, we visited Berlin and western Germany, now under military

occupation, and some of the countries which are members of the
Atlantic Pact. In all we visited 14 capitals and countries. . . . Our
trip was thoroughly organized in advance. The State Department
had charge of all diplomatic arrangements. The Military Department had charge of our transportation. Upon reaching a capital we
conferred first with our Ambassadors or Ministers and their staffs.
Second, we had conferences with the heads of the nation's government. Then we met and conferred with citizens and groups of
citizens interested in the welfare of their respective countries. We
made it plain to the heads of the several governments that we were
not there to meddle in their local affairs. Our instructions from
the Senate committee were to secure first-hand information in
each country with respect to the need for aid and assistance, and
then to ascertain just how the money already appropriated is being
expended.

"We found conditions in Europe much different from what we
expected. Some countries did not suffer materially in the recent
war and I refer to Sweden and Switzerland. Instead of suffering,
those two countries profited from the misfortune and destruction
of their neighbors. Some of the countries and areas visited are still
suffering beyond description. I refer to the city of Berlin and the
countries of Austria and Greece.

"Berlin, once a proud city of 4,000,000 people, is now a desert
waste of broken brick, stone, and rubble. Austria in eastern Europe,
and immediately adjacent to Russia, is under joint military occupation by Russia, England, France, and the United States. Vienna, the
capital, once famed for its culture, music, and art, now has the
appearance of rapidly approaching a ghost city. Greece, torn by
civil war, is in a bad condition; however, the Communist invaders
from the east have been defeated and Greece is now again free.

"Through the aid, assistance, and leadership of the United States,
a corridor has been built through central Europe, extending from
Norway on the north through Denmark, western Germany, Austria,

Italy, and Greece, and Turkey on the south. If Russia tries to extend
her present possessions either west or south, the countries forming
the corridor or wall must be pierced, and any attempt at aggression
by Russia will, in my opinion, mean certain war. To protect and
defend this corridor wall the nations adjacent to Russia must have
help, and such help is being furnished by the Marshall Plan and
Atlantic Pact appropriations.

"This Russian threat and menace now confronts the Allied Powers, the Congress, and the people of America. The world leadership
now in our hands is devoted to the task of organizing the countries
of western Europe for their own self-defense and for mutual cooperation and helpfulness. Not one of such countries, acting alone, is
able to offer any substantial resistance to an attack by Russia. They
realize that unless they pool their forces they may be taken over one
by one.

"It was our country that suggested the Marshall Plan. It was our
country that suggested the Atlantic Pact. The Marshall Plan calls for
the unification and consolidation of the manpower, the economy
and the military to the end that an attack upon any one of the
countries will be considered an attack upon all such countries,
including the United States. The Atlantic Pact calls for the arming
of the youth of western Europe so that if war comes they can fight
on their own soil, rather than to have to train our own boys, arm
and equip them, and then send them to Europe again to fight a
foreign war. If Russia can be made to understand that any further
aggression on her part against any of the countries of Europe will be
considered as an act of aggression against all such countries, then
we hope and believe that the Russian leaders will stop, look, and
listen. . . . To prevent war with Russia is the supreme task in which we
are now engaged. Personally, I can see no alternative to the program that has been developed and agreed upon, and if such program fails, then war to the end is inevitable.

"During the last session of the Congress I voted to reduce the

Marshall Plan aid by some half billion dollars and such estimates were reduced accordingly. In the coming session I shall point out where American money is being expended in Europe unnecessarily and I shall recommend and vote to eliminate some countries entirely from the program and, also, I shall recommend and vote to cut appropriations to other countries. Some of these European countries have nationalized many of their major industries. For example, England has nationalized her coal, railway, electric, cement, and insurance industries and now is trying to force the House of Lords to join the House of Commons in nationalizing the steel industry. When an industry is nationalized, as a rule it ceases to pay taxes but this is not the worst or the whole story. The English nationalized industries are all being operated at a loss — so that the English treasury is not only losing the taxes formerly collected, but in addition is being compelled to meet the deficits and losses incurred by the inefficient operation and management of such nationalized industries.

"Today our American taxpayers are being called upon, first, to rehabilitate the war-devastated areas of Europe; second, to assist in developing and equipping a military establishment in western Europe as a protection against Russian aggression; and, third, to pay deficits caused by the loss of taxes from nationalized industries. Speaking as a United States Senator in the 14 capitals of Europe, I made it plain that the American people are tired of having to finance and fight foreign wars and then after such wars are over of having to rebuild their cities, their industries, and to assist in the rehabilitation of their peoples. . . .

"There must be a possible plan for the prevention of war. . . . Our own country has suggested and is trying to develop the United Nations into a world tribunal of such influence and power that it may be able to hear, consider, and adjust international issues and problems without either the excuse or the necessity for war. . . . If we can check the spread of communism and confine this obnoxious economic and political system to Russia, then our American free-enterprise system will continue to operate as an example and model for other liberty-loving peoples everywhere.

"We tried to make our mission clear that we were not in Europe to meddle in the local affairs of any nation. In every country visited, I stated positively that we did not covet an acre of their land, and that we were not there to suggest any changes in their form of government or any changes in their way of life. Our delegation was received by the prime ministers and heads of the various governments, and where their parliaments were in session we were accorded special honors. The Parliaments of Belgium, Italy, and England admitted our delegation to their chambers.

"We were received and entertained by the Kings of Norway and Greece. In Norway, King Haakon gave us a luncheon in the palace. The King speaks English fluently and asked about America and was interested in Oklahoma. As I was taking my leave I said: 'Your Majesty, I extend to you an invitation to visit me in Oklahoma.' 'Oh,' said the King, 'I am too old to take such a trip.' I happened to know that he was just under 80, so I replied: 'Your Majesty, in Oklahoma life begins at 80.' To which the King replied: 'In that event, I shall think it over.'

"In Italy we were given a special audience by Pope Pius the Twelfth at his summer residence near Rome. For the Pope, let me say that he has the dignity of a king of kings—yet, at the same time, he is as democratic as the humblest citizen of our country. He had prepared a special address for our delegation. He spoke in English and approved of our mission to Europe and has thrown his vast influence and power on the side of the peoples who want to be free. He is our most valuable and powerful ally in this contest with godless Russia. . . .

"After the hearings on the various items of appropriations involving assistance and aid to foreign peoples, and after personal visits to the 14 Marshall aid and Atlantic Pact countries, I have come to the following conclusions: First, in the American and Allied program for checking the spread of communism, the most important point to receive consideration is the city of Berlin. From my viewpoint, Berlin is the keystone of the arch of the program for stopping the spread of communism in Europe. If we should, for any reason, move out of the picture in Berlin, then both England and France would have to follow because they are without power to remain in Berlin if we should decide to evacuate that city. If we should move out of Berlin, Russia would move in on the same day that we move out, and the same is true of western Germany. If we should decide to withdraw our military and civilian personnel from western Germany, then England and France would have to withdraw their forces. Such an event would give Russia complete possession and control of all of Germany. . . . In my opinion a voluntary withdrawal from Berlin and Germany would mean a forced withdrawal from all of Europe, because Russia has designs on taking over the entire continent of Europe.

"To date we have not lost this contest. On this issue our people are unified and not divided. The free peoples of the world are following our leadership. The American leadership belongs to no one political party. America and peoples who want to be free, when unified and working in a common cause and to a common end, cannot lose and suffer defeat.

"Our trip, from the beginning to the end, was most successful. We were received by most of the nations visited with almost pathetic gratitude. In Athens, Greece, the streets from the airport to the hotel were lined with thankful and appreciative people. In that country the United States is universally conceded to be their savior. Other European countries gave unmistakable evidence of their friendship for America. This cold war with Russia has been, and will continue to be expensive, but when we win—and with God's help we will win—whatever we have left after the victory will be just that much saved. . . ."

WHY I ENTERED PUBLIC SERVICE:
RETIREMENT REFLECTIONS

During my services as a legislator I was guided by a conviction that government was instituted and maintained to "promote the general welfare" of the people. To me this meant all the people and not just those few who could influence, dictate, or manage the affairs of government. Very early in life I learned that the Declaration of Independence contained a statement "that all men are created equal," yet I did not have to live long to become convinced that the equality was limited to "under the law" and did not apply to either equal ability, equal opportunity, or equal environment at birth and during childhood and youth. I did not enter the public service to try to alter, retard, or destroy the favorable opportunity and environment of the favored or lucky few, but instead I hoped to be able to help, at least in a small way, those who came into being handicapped by poverty and lack of opportunity. With my background, I could never forget the lack of environment and opportunity which confront the multiplied millions of boys and girls who are born, who live, and who die without a chance for even trying to help make the world a better place for those who are to come after them.

When I now reflect upon my tenure of legislative service, I can remember but few instances where those specially favored by environment and opportunity ever appealed to me for aid and assistance. In my early life I knew and came in contact with only those who had to work to keep the wolves from their doors. In so far as I knew, only farmers, laborers, and those who served the two groups existed; hence, I became convinced early that if government could help farmers and workers to enjoy a degree of prosperity, then those who live off those two groups would not need special attention and consideration.

To my way of thinking farmers not only need but must have fair prices for the things they produce, and workers must likewise have jobs at fair wages if the other groups of our people are to have prosperity. From history . . . it is obvious that when farmers have fair prices and workers have jobs at fair wages, then all others have a chance to share in such prosperity, but when the masses of the people are impoverished, then the other groups which serve the masses soon suffer adversity.

Always, I was obsessed with the belief and conviction that if I could do something to help farmers and workers, that by such accomplishments I would be helping all other groups of our people. With such convictions I had opportunities to try to help those I always carried in my conscience as needing assistance. Farmers held my first allegiance and wage earners were considered equally worthy of assistance. Our few hundred thousands of Indians, because of their enforced reliance upon the government, were never voluntarily either forgotten or neglected. It was upon the convictions and principles outlined herein that I carried on my legislative activities in my state of Oklahoma and in the national Congress.

When I retired from the Senate on January 3, 1951, I realized that, after a service of four years in the House and twenty-four in the Senate, I had less money than when I entered the Congress twenty-eight years before. Then it dawned upon me that I had been serving the public for over a quarter of a century for my "board and keep." While serving as a legislator, in addition to expenses, my real compensation came from a realization that the office enabled me to do things for people that they could not do for themselves.

During the early years of my public service, the expenses of making campaigns were not heavy. My campaigns for the State Senate cost but little. The expenses of making campaigns for the national House of Representatives cost more, but only relatively, as the district was larger. In the early days while campaigning for the State Senate and for Congress, I paid all my expenses. In my first campaign for the U.S. Senate in 1926, I paid all primary campaign expenses; however, in the general election the State Democratic Central Committee financed the campaign for the state ticket.

In my second primary campaign in 1932 but little money was expended. Times were hard, prices were low, and money was scarce; hence, my opponents did not conduct expensive campaigns. I made but one trip to the state, made one statewide radio speech, made a few public appearances, and used little space in the papers for advertising my candidacy. As stated, the campaign was made during the depression; hence, my arguments in the main were leveled against the opposition party, which at that time had been in power for 12 years. In Oklahoma the results of the campaign were not at any time in doubt.

By 1938, when my third campaign came on, statewide political campaigns had developed into "big business." Under the Oklahoma law a candidate for the United States Senate was limited to an expenditure of $3,000 and with such a limited sum it was impossible to make a respectable statewide contest. In my prior contests my opposition did not spend much money, so that with my advantage of being already in office and with the franking privilege, I was able to get by within the limits of the law.

The franking privilege is valuable on account of the fact that a congressman or senator may have his speeches printed at the Government Printing Office at cost for paper and labor and then he may mail such printed matter to the voters at no cost for postage. Under the limitations of the Oklahoma law, candidates were compelled when real opposition developed to permit their friends and supporters to form committees to plan campaigns and then to finance such contests. When I personally made my own plans and paid my own expenses, Mrs. Thomas, my wife, was my campaign manager.

In my third try for the Senate, times had so changed and campaigns had so developed that my friends insisted that we follow the new campaign technique by forming committees, collecting funds,

Thomas introduces President Franklin D. Roosevelt in Oklahoma City during the 1938 campaign. Thomas was seeking a third term in the U.S. Senate. Courtesy Carl Albert Center Congressional Archives, University of Oklahoma.

and conducting a regular Oklahoma form of statewide campaign. My opponents had set the pattern and it seemed necessary for me to conform or to perhaps suffer defeat.

My friends organized the committees. First, a statewide central organization was set up and then county committees were formed with managers in charge. As a rule the county committee raised their own funds and conducted their own campaigns; however, the state committee looked after such matters as erecting billboards, getting out campaign posters and literature, advertising in statewide newspapers, and then following up with personal campaigning, such as radio speeches, personal correspondence, widespread circular mailing, and speeches by the candidate and by his supporters.

In 1938 President Roosevelt was serving his second term and, having worked out of the depression, was at the height of power and popularity. It was under the law which I prepared and sponsored in 1933 that the president was able to increase commodity prices and bring about better times. In fact, by 1937 the general price level had so increased that the administration had taken steps to check the advance in prices. Since his election I had worked with and supported the president, so in my campaign for re-election he volunteered to visit Oklahoma in my behalf. The trip was made on Saturday before the primary election on the following Tuesday. Vast crowds at Oklahoma City lined the streets leading to the fair grounds where the president made his main address of the day. . . . While the primary campaign was already won, the visit of President Roosevelt did much to increase the majority and then to insure success at the November election.

In my 1944 campaign for re-election to the Senate, World War Two was on and it was difficult to develop interest in political contests. However, the fact that the campaign was for the election of a president brought out a large vote in the November election. In the face of active opposition I won the nomination and the election by the usual majorities.

Then came my try for a fifth term in the Senate. . . . In 1950, my public service covered over 41 years and this fact was used by my opposition as the main argument for my retirement. The fact that under the congressional set-up the older members who had served longest had the highest places on the several committees made little impression on many voters. . . .

SENIORITY

Oftentimes I have been asked respecting the benefits to a state of retaining its senators and congressmen in office as long as they will consent to serve. To one who served in the Senate long enough to become the third-ranking member among the total of 96, long enough to become chairman of the Committee on Agriculture and Forestry, and also long enough to become second in line on the all important Committee on Appropriations, I was in a position to give an answer which I think would be concurred in by all who have had membership in "the greatest deliberative legislative body in the world."

The senators having seniority, meaning longer service, have the committees of their choice. In my case, I represented Oklahoma — a farm state; hence, my first choice was that of agriculture. Then my state being new and with many federal institutions and interests, my second choice was appropriations. Our many Indian tribes, reservations, agencies, schools, and hospitals; our military establishments, such as Fort Reno and Fort Sill; our public reservations, such as the Platt National Park and the Wichita Mountains Wildlife Refuge; and the state's great need for flood control and irrigation projects made it mandatory, in my opinion, that Oklahoma should have a representative on the Appropriations Committee. New members, as a rule, cannot secure membership on the more important committees during their first few years in the Senate.

Mere membership on the more important committees is not the most important part of the service. In the enactment of important legislation very often different viewpoints are entertained by the respective houses of the Congress. When a bill is passed by one house, it must go to the other house for consideration and action. If differences develop between the House and Senate, the only way an agreement may be reached is for each house to appoint what is

known as a "conference committee" and then refer the disagree-
ment between the houses to such committees for adjustment.

In appointing such conference committees, the rule is that the
chairman and ranking members of the committees having jurisdiction of the subject matter in each house are named as conferees.
Thus members not on such committees have no chance to serve on
such conferences. Also, members on the respective committees
with little seniority as a rule do not have a chance to work out
agreements to the end that a law may be perfected and passed.

It is a fact that much of the important legislation is written by the
members of the conference committees. When an agreement is
reached and the bill is amended to include such adjustment, then
the bill is reported to the respective houses for acceptance or re-
jection. A conference committee report may not be amended or
changed but must be voted up or down exactly as presented. If the
bill, as amended, is rejected, then, as a rule it is ordered re-referred
to the same conferees, sometimes with instructions covering the
objections which caused the report to be turned down; hence, it is
clear that in the preparation and enactment of much of the important legislation new members can be little more than interested
spectators. . . .

To show the concrete results of seniority, or long service, in the
Congress we could cite many illustrations, but a few are typical of
all. Kenneth McKellar of Tennessee, being the senator at present
with the longest service, is president pro tempore of the Senate and
also is chairman of the Committee on Appropriations. Only in rare
instances does a senator ascend to either position much short of a
quarter of a century of continuous service. As president pro tempore, Senator McKellar presides over the Senate in the absence of
the vice-president, and as chairman of the Appropriations Committee he supervises the allocation and expenditure of the billions of
dollars appropriated to pay the bills of the greatest nation on earth.

Because of his long service and his power resulting therefrom, he was able to secure for his state the location of the government's experiment in the development and distribution of public power, known as the Tennessee Valley Authority.[72] This project has meant an expenditure already of approximately $1 billion of public funds in the development of the natural resources of not only the state of Tennessee but of adjacent states. In fact Senator McKellar has secured so many projects and institutions for his state that his colleagues wonder where he finds sites for the dams, reservoirs, steam-generating plants, research laboratories, and innumerable factories being located in Tennessee. . . . It was due to my seniority on the Committee on Agriculture that in 1933 I was able to have approved an amendment to a farm bill which gave the president the power to revalue the dollar, thereby raising prices, and at the same time making a profit to the Treasury on the gold removed from each dollar in a total sum of $2.8 billion. . . .

After more than 40 years in legislative work, and without hope of further public service, I make the following recommendation with respect to service in the Congress: Constituencies should exercise their very best judgment in the selection of congressmen and senators in the first instance, and then when an official is once nominated and elected, they should keep such congressman or senator in office so long as he faithfully and honestly represents the best interests of his district or state. It is to be expected that heavy industrial areas should be represented by congressmen sympathetic to the best interests of labor; and that agricultural districts and states should be represented by congressmen and senators sympathetic to the best interests of farmers. It is obvious that when wage earners and farmers are prosperous all others have an opportunity to share in the general prosperity.

With respect to every issue developed, considered from every standpoint, domestic, national, and international, there is always a best solution. The older congressmen and senators, with vast store-

houses of pertinent information and experienced in solving economic and legislative problems, have every opportunity and advantage to suggest and provide the text of legislation necessary to meet
the issue and to solve the problem. Due to the intricate parliamentary rules, procedures, and practices, and in view of the vast and
rapidly expanding interests of the United States, it is too much to
expect that new congressmen and senators will be able to wield
much power and influence in either house of the Congress during
their early years of service. If an official has energy, ability, and
education, defined as qualifications, and then has . . . an all out
desire to serve the public, then the longer such congressman or
senator is retained in office, the more efficient, the more powerful,
and the more valuable he will be to his district or state. Districts and
states which keep their representatives in Congress are able to practically control legislation.

In writing the Constitution, the Founding Fathers gave first place
of importance to the legislative branch of the government. Some 65
percent of the text is devoted to the powers of the Congress and the
balance of 35 percent is divided between the judicial and executive
branches. In our federal set-up the Congress makes the policies, the
courts interpret such policies, and the administrative branch ex-
ecutes the laws as passed and interpreted.

This all means that those who control the Congress, in effect,
control the government. It further means that the congressmen
and senators with the longest seniority have the committee chair-
manships and ranking positions on all committees. Presidents, cabinet members, and bureau chiefs come and go, but the districts and
states which keep their congressmen and senators in office seem-
ingly go on forever, and in reality such senators and congressmen
control the government of the United States. Districts and states
which change their congressmen and senators about every opportunity must be content with services and results comparable to services and results available to territories just admitted to statehood.

My public service as a legislator began with statehood for Oklahoma on November 16, 1907, and ended with the close of the Eighty-first Congress on January 3, 1951. This service was continuous and unbroken save for the period 1920 to 1922. At the end of my long tenure of service my colleague from Oklahoma, Senator Robert S. Kerr,[73] paid me the following tribute on the floor of the Senate.

"I wish to pay a brief but sincere tribute to Elmer Thomas, my colleague and the retiring Senator from Oklahoma, who will be leaving us at the end of this session. . . . As a new member in the Senate two years ago, I greatly profited from his advice and counsel and I have always profoundly appreciated his kindness in extending to me the benefit of his wisdom and experience gained from many years of devoted and valued service in the Senate. . . .

"His career of public service to his State and to his Nation began early in life. When he was only 19 years old he exhibited a remarkable ability and interest in national affairs. At this youthful age he made 28 speeches in Indiana, where he was born, in support of the candidacy of William Jennings Bryan for President. This same resourceful spirit continued when he set out on his own to go West to Oklahoma in 1900. In Oklahoma, as in Indiana, his political sagacity soon won for him a prominent place in the Democratic Party and in the government of that State.

"He was elected to the State Senate at the time Oklahoma was granted statehood in 1907, and served in that capacity until he ran for Congress in 1920. He was elected as a member of the House of Representatives to the 68th and 69th Congresses and in 1926 he was elected to the Senate. His membership in both Houses of Congress he regarded as one of the highest attainments in American life, and he worked diligently to live up to the responsibilities and demands of this high office.

"The farmers in our nation never had a friend who was more devoted to their welfare, sincere in serving their economic needs. Having served on the Committee on Agriculture for more than

Secretary of Agriculture Charles F. Brannon (right) confers with Senator Thomas, chair of the Senate Agriculture Committee, about the
department's plan not to include acreage planted to wheat and cotton
for 1949 harvesting in quota allocations. Courtesy U.S. Senate Historical Office.

20 years, he is perhaps one of the most outstanding authorities in
the country on agricultural problems and requirements of the
American farmer.

"In 1938, he helped develop and pass a law creating the Rural
Electrification Administration.[74] As a high-ranking member of the
Appropriations Committee he has sought liberal appropriations to
expand this program. With the recent allotments granted for rural
power loans by the REA last month, the States will have available
over 141 million dollars for the expansion of rural power systems.
Under these state allocations, Oklahoma will have available the

third largest amount among the states, having over 9 million dollars at its disposal.

"His deep interest in flood control and his comprehensive knowledge of every phase of our farm economy has exerted a great influence on the agricultural legislation of the last two decades. Through his unceasing efforts for flood control legislation, he has not only improved the plight of the farmer, but fostered and encouraged industrialization in a large area of our country which had previously lacked cheap power facilities. . . .

"In addition to his vigorous support of higher prices for the farmer's products, he had the vision and intelligence to sponsor a provision by which surplus farm products are distributed to the needy people of our nation. His keen perception and ability to grasp the problem and needs of the people from an all inclusive viewpoint is indicative of his ordered mind and the unique faculty of seeing the dependence of one phase of American life upon the other. . . . His long and distinguished career as a true statesman and a great legislator should be a challenge to all of us and an inspiration to the youth of America."

Notes

INTRODUCTION

1. James Scales and Danney Goble, *Oklahoma Politics: A History* (Norman: University of Oklahoma Press, 1982), 139.

2. Elmer Thomas, *Financial Engineering* (Washington, D.C.: privately published, 1953). Elmer Thomas, *Autobiography of an Enigma* (New York: Pageant Press, 1965).

FORTY YEARS A LEGISLATOR

1. Jackson's company, which became the Southwestern Land and Loan Company, was a prominent real estate firm. See the *Daily Oklahoman*, October 5, 1901, p. 6, and March 10, 1907, p. 66, for information about both companies.

2. For accounts of the land lottery, see Edward Everett Dale, *Oklahoma: The Story of a State* (Evanston, Ill.: Row, Peterson and Company, 1958), 248–51. Dale cogently explains the reasons for the shift from land runs to lotteries. For a fuller account with ample information about James R. Woods and Mattie Beal, see *The History of Comanche County* (Lawton, Okla.): Southwest Oklahoma Genealogical Society, 1985), 18–27; Gaston Litton, *History of Oklahoma: At the Golden Anniversary of Statehood* (New York: Lewis Historical Publishing Company, 1957), 1: 402–404; A. Emma Estill, "The Great Lottery, August 6, 1901," *Chronicles of Oklahoma* 9 (December 1931): 365–81; B. B. Chapman, "Land Office Business at Lawton and El Reno," *Great*

Plains Journal 7 (1967): 1–25. The Museum of the Great Plains in Lawton has a collection of Mattie Beal's papers; material about James R. Woods can be found in the Darryl P. Greenwood Collection.

3. A post office for Medicine Park was established on October 13, 1908. See Linda Paulson Branson, "The Evolution of a Resort Community: Medicine Park, Oklahoma" (M.A. thesis, University of Oklahoma, 1992); and Thomas Selland and H. Eren Erdener, eds., *Medicine Park, Oklahoma* (Norman: University of Oklahoma College of Environmental Design, Center for Environmental Design and Research, 1981). This latter volume devotes much attention to buildings and structures, including rock homes.

4. James H. Howard II, "Charles Nathaniel Haskell, 1907–1911," in LeRoy H. Fischer, ed., *Oklahoma's Governors, 1907–1929: Turbulent Politics* (Oklahoma City: Oklahoma Historical Society, 1981), 20–46.

5. Kenny Brown, "A Progressive from Oklahoma: Senator Robert Latham Owen, Jr.," *Chronicles of Oklahoma* 62 (Fall 1984): 232–65; and Edward Elmer Keso, *The Senatorial Career of Robert Latham Owen* (Nashville: George Peabody College for Teachers, 1938).

6. Monroe Billington, *Thomas P. Gore: Blind Senator from Oklahoma* (Lawrence: University of Kansas Press, 1967).

7. For further information on the first Oklahoma Legislature, see James Scales and Danney Goble, *Oklahoma Politics: A History* (Norman: University of Oklahoma Press, 1982), 36–40.

8. Bobby Dean Smith, "Lee Cruce: Governor of Oklahoma, 1911–1915," in Fischer, *Oklahoma's Governors*, 47–65; Scales and Goble, *Oklahoma Politics*, 51–58. In addition see Orben J. Casey, "Governor Lee Cruce, White Supremacy and Capital Punishment, 1911–1915," *Chronicles of Oklahoma* 52 (Winter 1974–1975): 456–75 and Orben J. Casey, "Governor Lee Cruce and Law Enforcement, 1911–1915," *Chronicles of Oklahoma* 54 (Winter 1976–1977): 435–60.

9. Edward Everett Dale and James P. Morrison, *Pioneer Judge: The Life of Robert Lee Williams* (Cedar Rapids, Iowa: Torch Press, 1958); and Thomas A. Hazell, "Robert Lee Williams, Governor of Oklahoma, 1915–1919," in Fischer, *Oklahoma's Governors*, 66–86. See, too, Scales and Goble, *Oklahoma Politics*, chapter 4 and part of chapter 5, pp. 80–90 for information on Williams's tenure as governor.

10. Jimmie L. White, Jr., "James Brooks Ayers Robertson: Governor of Oklahoma, 1919–1923," in Fischer, *Oklahoma's Governors*, 87–114; and Scales and Goble, *Oklahoma Politics*, pp. 90–96.

11. Senator E. P. Hill (1918–1922), a resident of McAlester, later played a prominent role in the preparation of the articles of impeachment of Governor Henry Simpson Johnston in 1927. Scales and Goble dub him one of the "Four Horsemen" seeking to unseat Johnston (*Oklahoma Politics,* 142). For a further account of the Hill-Thomas debate, see the *Daily Oklahoman,* April 29, 1919, p. 8.

12. Senator R. L. Davidson (1916–22) from Tulsa was Democratic state chairman during the tenure of Governor John Calloway Walton. Previously during Governor Robertson's administration, he was president pro tempore of the Senate. See the *Daily Oklahoman,* May 2, 1919, p. 20, for an account of the Thomas-Davidson debate in Muskogee.

13. Carl Williams became editor of the *Oklahoma Farmer-Stockman* in 1913. By the 1920s, he was regarded as one of the more influential individuals in American agriculture. He was an organizer of the American Cotton Exchange and in 1929 was appointed by President Herbert Hoover as a member of the Federal Farm Board.

14. Colonel Roy Hoffman was a prominent Spanish-American War veteran. He later commanded the National Guard of Oklahoma, served as Brigadier-General in World War One, and in 1931 was made a Major General and commander of the 45th Division, National Guard.

15. M. L. Turner was president of the Western National Bank in Oklahoma City.

16. With statehood, Henry M. Furman was appointed presiding judge of the Criminal Court of Appeals.

17. Upon admission of Oklahoma as a state, Scott Ferris was elected as a Democrat to the 60th Congress and served from November 16, 1907, until March 3, 1921. An entry delineating his service can be found in the *Biographical Directory of the American Congress, 1774–2005* (Washington, D.C.: Government Printing Office, 2005). Hereafter, when no published information on a member of Congress is readily available, an entry will be found in the *Biographical Directory* and the member's name will not be cited in the notes.

18. Maynard J. Hanson, "Senator William B. Pine and His Times" (Ph.D. dissertation, Oklahoma State University, 1983); and Stephen Jones, *Once Before: The Political and Senatorial Careers of Oklahoma's First Two Republican United States Senators: John W. Harreld and W. B. Pine* (Enid, Okla.: Dougherty Press, 1983).

19. See Jones, *Once Before.*

20. Anthony Champagne, *Congressman Sam Rayburn* (New Brunswick,

N.J.: Rutgers University Press, 1984); and D. B. Hardeman and Donald C. Bacon, *Rayburn: A Biography* (Austin: Texas Monthly Press, 1987).

21. For the 1924 decision, see *State of Oklahoma v. State of Texas*, 265 U.S. 493. Justice Willis Van Devanter delivered the opinion of the Court. See also the *Daily Oklahoman*, April 26, 1922, p. 1 and January 16, 1923, p. 16.

22. For more on this project, see Monroe Billington, "W. C. Austin Irrigation Project," *Chronicles of Oklahoma* 30 (Summer 1952): 207–15 and Monroe Billington, "W. C. Austin: Pioneer and Public Servant," *Chronicles of Oklahoma* 31 (Spring 1953): 66–75. The latter provides a biographical sketch. Austin was the first president of the Oklahoma Reclamation Association.

23. For more on this vast project, see W. R. Holway, "Dams on the Grand River," *Chronicles of Oklahoma* 26 (Autumn 1948): 329–34.

24. For further information on these mineral lands, see Michael J. Hightower, "Cattle, Coal and Indian Land: A Tradition of Mining in Southeastern Oklahoma," *Chronicles of Oklahoma* 62 (Spring 1984): 4–25.

25. For two important volumes that discuss the Bonus March and the key players, see Roger Daniels, *The Bonus March: An Episode of the Great Depression* (Westport, Conn.: Greenwood Publishing Company, 1971); and Donald J. Lisio, *The President and Protest: Hoover, MacArthur, and the Bonus Riot* (New York: Fordham University Press, 1994). For stories on Walter W. Waters, see *Daily Oklahoman*, June 21, 1932, p. 3, and June 30, 1932, p. 4.

26. For more information on Wright Patman, see Nancy Beck Young's prize-winning *Wright Patman: Populism, Liberalism, and the American Dream* (Dallas: Southern Methodist University Press, 2000).

27. Evans C. Johnson, "John H. Bankhead 2d: Advocate of Cotton," *Alabama Review* 41 (January 1988): 430–58; and Jack Brien Key, "John H. Bankhead, Jr., of Alabama: The Conservative as Reformer" (Ph.D. dissertation, Johns Hopkins University, 1966).

28. Milton R. Morrill, *Reed Smoot: Apostle in Politics* (Logan: Utah State University Press, 1990); James B. Allen, "The Great Protectionist: Senator Reed Smoot of Utah," *Utah Historical Quarterly* 45 (Fall 1977): 325–45.

29. For an older but still useful study, see Joseph M. Jones, *Tariff Retaliation: Repercussions of the Hawley-Smoot Bill* (Philadelphia: University of Pennsylvania Press, 1934; reprinted New York: Garland Publishing, 1983); E. E. Schattschneider, *Politics, Pressures and the Tariff: A Study of Free Private Enterprise in Pressure Politics, as Shown in the 1929–1930 Revision of the Tariff* (New York: Prentice-Hall, 1935); J. Richard Snyder, "Hoover and the Hawley-

Smoot Tariff: A View of Executive Leadership," *Annals of Iowa* 41 (1973): 1173–89; C. Edward Petty, "Foreign Retaliation to the Smoot-Hawley Tariff" (M.A. thesis, University of Oklahoma, 1943).

30. Walter E. Edge, *A Jerseyman's Journal: Fifty Years of American Business and Politics* (Princeton: Princeton University Press, 1948; reprinted New York: Johnson Reprint, 1972).

31. See the obituary notice in *Daily Oklahoman,* January 14, 1959, p. 26.

32. Wirt Franklin, president of the Independent Petroleum Association of American from 1929 to 1935, is the subject of a biographical entry in Litton, *History of Oklahoma,* 4: 618–20. In 1932, Franklin was defeated in his bid to join Thomas as a colleague in the U.S. Senate. For his activities early in the New Deal when Secretary of the Interior Harold Ickes consulted with him about the oil industry, see Harold Ickes, *The Secret Diary of Harold L. Ickes: The First Thousand Days* (New York: Simon and Schuster, 1953).

33. Horace Adams, "Thaddeus H. Caraway in the United States Senate" (Ph.D. dissertation, George Peabody College for Teachers, 1935).

34. J. Leonard Bates, *Senator Thomas J. Walsh of Montana: Law and Public Affairs, From TR to FDR* (Urbana: University of Illinois Press, 1999).

35. Patrick O'Brien, "Senator J. J. Blaine: An Independent Progressive during 'Normalcy,'" *Wisconsin Magazine of History* 60 (Autumn 1976): 25–41.

36. Martin Ewy, "Charles Curtis of Kansas, Vice President of the United States, 1929–1933," *Emporia State Research Studies* 10 (December 1961): 5–58.

37. James Eli Watson, *As I Knew Them: Memoirs of James R. Watson, Former United States Senator from Indiana* (Indianapolis: Bobbs-Merrill, 1936).

38. At this time Hard was, as a political correspondent, supplying Washington dispatches to the Consolidated Press Association and to weekly and monthly periodicals.

39. George Sanford Holmes was the Washington correspondent of the *Rocky Mountain News, Birmingham Post,* and *Oklahoma News.*

40. Allan H. Meltzer, *A History of the Federal Reserve,* vol. 1, *1913–1951* (Chicago: University of Chicago Press, 2003); Milton Friedman and Anna Jacobson Schwartz, *A Monetary History of the United States, 1867–1960* (Princeton: Princeton University Press, 1963). Meltzer, like Thomas, carefully traced the importance of Federal Reserve policy in the development of the Great Depression and the effect of monetary policy on business cycles and price stability. Friedman and Schwartz argued in their history that the

Federal Reserve Board's error was to let the money supply shrink while the
real economy was imploding, a point Thomas would have had no difficulty
in accepting.

41. Keith L. Bryant, *Alfalfa Bill Murray* (Norman: University of Oklahoma Press, 1968); Francis W. Schruben, "The Return of Alfalfa Bill Murray," *Chronicles of Oklahoma* 41 (Spring 1963): 38–65.

42. See Lester Vernon Chandler, *Benjamin Strong, Central Banker* (Wash-
ington, D.C.: Brookings Institution, 1958). Strong was head of the New
York Federal Reserve Bank, see Silvano A. Wueschner, *Charting Twentieth
Century Monetary Policy: Herbert Hoover and Benjamin Strong, 1917–1927*
(Westport, Conn.: Greenwood Press, 1999); and Laurence Edmund Clark,
*Central Banking Under the Federal Reserve System, with Special Consideration of the
Federal Reserve Bank of New York* (New York: Macmillan, 1935).

43. Anderson, Buckner, Maxwell, and Hayden were prominent in the
New York banking community. Harriss was a leading cotton broker, and
Burgess the chief economist at the New York Federal Reserve Bank.

44. Burton K. Wheeler, *Yankee from the West: The Candid, Turbulent Life
Story of the Yankee-Born U.S. Senator from Montana* (Garden City, N.Y.: Doubleday, 1962; reprinted New York: Octagon Books, 1977).

45. Arthur M. Johnson, *Winthrop W. Aldrich: Lawyer, Banker, Diplomat*
(Boston: Harvard University Press, 1968).

46. Rixey Smith and Norman Beasley, *Carter Glass: A Biography* (New
York: Longmans, Green and Company, 1939; reprinted New York: Da Capo
Press, 1972); Alfred C. Koeniger, " 'Unreconstructed Rebel': The Political
Thought and Senate Career of Carter Glass, 1929–1936" (Ph.D. disserta-
tion, Vanderbilt University, 1980).

47. For an obituary notice on Woodin, who served less than a year as
Secretary of the Treasury, see the *Daily Oklahoman*, May 4, 1934, p. 1.

48. Wayne Flynt, *Duncan Upshaw Fletcher, Dixie's Reluctant Progressive* (Tal-
lahassee: Florida State University Press, 1971).

49. Elliot A. Rosen, *Roosevelt, the Great Depression, and the Economics of
Recovery* (Charlottesville: University Press of Virginia, 2005). Rosen provides a superb account exploring the causes of the Great Depression and
America's recovery by focusing on policies and policy alternatives in play
during the New Deal, disentangling economic claims from political ideol-
ogy. Chapters 2 and 3 ("Nationalizing the Economy" and "Dollar Devalua-
tion and the Monetary Group") place Thomas, whom Rosen mentions,
within the context of the policy debates at the outset of the New Deal.

50. *Norman v. Baltimore & Ohio Railroad Co.; United States v. Bankers Trust Co.,* and *Nortz v. United States*—popularly called the "Gold Clause Cases"—were disposed in opinions handed down on February 18, 1935, by Chief Justice Charles Evans Hughes. See 294 U.S. 240 and 294 U.S. 330. For a brief discussion, see Paul Finkelman and Melvin Urofsky, *Landmark Decisions of the United States Supreme Court* (Washington, D.C.: CQ Press, 2003), 196–97; John P. Dawson, "The Gold Clause Decisions," *Michigan Law Review* 33 (1935): 647.

51. Thomas Bassett Macaulay in 1934 was chairman of the board of directors of the Sun Life Assurance Company of Canada. Previously, he had served a term as president of the Actuarial Society of America.

52. Raymond Potter, "Royal S. Copeland, 1868–1938: A Physician in Politics" (Ph.D. dissertation, Case Western Reserve University, 1967).

53. Forrest Pogue, in his magisterial four-volume biography, discusses the general's career during the prewar years in vol. 2, *Ordeal and Hope, 1939–1942* (New York: Viking Press, 1965).

54. Thomas M. Coffee, *HAP: The Story of the U.S. Air Force and the Man Who Built It: General Henry H. "Hap" Arnold* (New York: Viking Press, 1982).

55. Keith Eiler, *Mobilizing America: Robert Patterson and the War Effort, 1940–1945* (Ithaca: Cornell University Press, 1997).

56. Bascom Timmons, *Jesse Jones, the Man and the Statesman* (New York: Holt, 1956; reprinted Westport, Conn.: Greenwood Press, 1975). See also the superb essay on Jones in Jordan Schwarz, *The New Dealers: Power Politics in the Age of Roosevelt* (New York: Vintage Books, 1994).

57. Ross R. Rice, *Carl Hayden: Builder of the American West* (Lanham, Md.: University Press of America, 1994).

58. Godfrey Hodgson, *The Colonel: The Life and Wars of Henry Stimson, 1867–1950* (Boston: Northeastern University Press, 1992); Elting E. Morison, *Turmoil and Tradition: A Study of the Life and Times of Henry L. Stimson* (Boston: Houghton Mifflin, 1960).

59. Alben Barkley, *That Reminds Me* (Garden City, N.Y.: Doubleday, 1954); James K. Libbey, *Dear Alben: Mr. Barkley of Kentucky* (Lexington: University Press of Kentucky, 1979); Donald A. Ritchie, "Alben Barkley: The President's Man," in Richard A. Baker and Roger H. Davidson, eds., *First among Equals: Outstanding Senate Majority Leaders of the Twentieth Century* (Washington, D.C.: Congressional Quarterly, 1991): 127–62.

60. G. Paschal Zachary, *Endless Frontier: Vannevar Bush, Engineer of the American Century* (Cambridge, Mass.: MIT Press, 1999); Vannevar Bush,

Modern Arms and Free Men: A Discussion of the Role of Science in Preserving Democracy (New York: Simon and Schuster, 1949).

61. Robert Dean Pope, "Senatorial Baron: The Long Political Career of Kenneth C. McKellar" (Ph.D. dissertation, Yale University, 1975).

62. As a major general, Frank Lowe became President Truman's "eyes and ears" in Korea during the Korean War.

63. As a brigadier general, Harry Vaughn became President Truman's military aide.

64. Lester I. Gordon, "John McCormack and the Roosevelt Era" (Ph.D. dissertation, Boston University, 1976).

65. William A. Hasenfus, "Managing Partner: Joseph W. Martin, Jr., Republican Leader of the United States House of Representatives, 1939–1959" (Ph.D. dissertation, Boston College, 1986); Joseph W. Martin and Robert J. Donovan, *My First Fifty Years in Politics* (New York: McGraw-Hill, 1960).

66. James J. Kiepper, *Styles Bridges: Yankee Senator* (Sugar Hill, N.H.: Phoenix, 2001).

67. Lt. General Thomas T. Handy was deputy chief of staff.

68. William Lawren, *The General and the Bomb: A Biography of General Leslie L. Groves, Director of the Manhattan Project* (N.Y.: Dodd, Mead, 1988).

69. Michele Stenehjem Gerber, *On the Home Front: The Cold War Legacy of the Hanford Nuclear Site*, 2nd. Ed. (Lincoln: University of Nebraska Press, 2002); *Hanford Site Historic District: History of Plutonium Production Facilities, 1943–1990* (Columbus: Battelle Press, 2003).

70. Supreme Court Justice Robert Jackson was chief United States prosecutor. Attorney General Francis Biddle was the American judge on the tribunal. Francis Biddle, *In Brief Authority* (Westport, Conn.: Greenwood Press, 1976); Eugene C. Gerhart, *America's Advocate: Robert H. Jackson* (Indianapolis: Bobbs-Merrill, 1958). See also, among numerous other studies, Whitney R. Harris, *Tyranny on Trial: The Trial of the Major German War Criminals at the End of World War II at Nuremberg, Germany, 1945–1946* (Dallas: Southern Methodist University Press, 1999); and Ann Tusa and John Tusa, *The Nuremberg Trial* (New York: Atheneum, 1984).

71. John H. Backer, *Winds of History: The German Years of Lucius DuBignon Clay* (New York: Van Nostrand Reinhold, 1983); Jean Edward Smith, *Lucius D. Clay: An American Life* (New York: Henry Holt, 1990).

72. Erwin C. Hargrove, *TVA: Fifty Years of Grass-roots Bureaucracy* (Urbana: University of Illinois Press, 1983); Thomas K. McCraw, *TVA and the Power*

Fight, 1933–1939 (Philadelphia: Lippincott, 1971); Gordon Clapp, *The TVA* (Chicago: University of Chicago Press, 1955); and Walter Creese, *TVA's Public Planning: The Vision, the Reality* (Knoxville: University of Tennessee Press, 1990).

73. Anne Hodges Morgan, *Robert S. Kerr: The Senate Years* (Norman: University of Oklahoma Press, 1977).

74. Marquis Childs, *The Farmer Takes a Hand: The Electric Power Revolution in Rural America* (Garden City, N.Y.: Doubleday, 1952); D. Clayton Brown, *Electricity for Rural America: The Fight for the REA* (Westport, Conn.: Greenwood Press, 1980).

Index

Pius XII, 151
Platt National Park (Okla.), 158

Rayburn, Sam, 30, 129
Reconstruction Finance Corporation,
    67, 117
Red River, oil under riverbed, 30–34
Reed, David A., 61, 69–70
Ribbentrop, Joachim von, 144
Richards, George, 122, 129, 135
Richland Village, Wash., 136
Roads, 25–26, 47, 49–50
Robertson, James B. A., 25
Roosevelt, Franklin D., 35–36, 39, 46,
    80, 88, 90–92, 95–96, 103, 106, 115,
    157
Roosevelt, Theodore, 15
Rural Electrification Administration,
    163

Saturday Evening Post, article entitled
    "The Origins of the Banking Panic of
    March 4, 1933," 88
Scott, Mount (Okla.), 10
Seniority, Thomas's reflections on,
    158–61
Sinnott, Nicholas J., 33
Smith, Edith. *See* Thomas, Edith
Smoot, Reed, 57, 59–60
Standard Oil Company of New Jersey, 61
State Capitol Commission, 21
Stimson, Henry L., 120–23, 128–30

Tennessee Valley Authority, 41, 160
Thomas, Edith, 8, 155
Thomas, Wilford Smith, 8
Thye, Edward, 147
Trent, Dover P., 36
Truman, Harry, 127–28
Tulsa, Okla., 25
Turkey Creek (Okla.), 34
Turner, M. L. 27

Vaughn, Harry, 127
Veterans, 50–58

Wallgren, Monrad, 127
Walsh, Thomas J., 62–63
Water, in southwestern Oklahoma, 9–
    13
Waters, Walter W., 53
Watson, James E., 66–67
W. C. Austin Project, 36–38
Welch, Earl, 45
Wheeler, Burton K., 86, 95
White, Wallace H., 120–21, 129
Wichita Forest Reserve, 9
Wichita Mountains, 8–10
Wichita Mountains Wildlife Refuge, 158
Wiggin, Albert, 86
Williams, Carl, 25
Williams, Robert L., 21–22
Woodin, William, 96
Woods, James R., 7

Other books by Richard Lowitt

A Merchant Prince of the Nineteenth Century: William E. Dodge (New York, 1954)

George W. Norris: The Making of a Progressive, 1861–1912 (Syracuse, 1963; Westport, Conn., 1980)

The Truman-MacArthur Controversy (Chicago, 1967)

George W. Norris: The Persistence of a Progressive, 1913–1933 (Urbana, Ill., 1971)

George W. Norris: The Triumph of a Progressive, 1933–1944 (Urbana, Ill., 1978)

Bronson M. Cutting: Progressive Politician (Albuquerque, 1992)

The New Deal and the West (Bloomington, Ind., 1984; Norman, Okla., 1993)

Fred Harris: His Journey from Liberalism to Populism (Lanham, Md., 2002)

(with Valerie Sherer Mathes) *The Standing Bear Controversy: Prelude to Indian Reform* (Urbana, Ill., 2003)

American Outback: The Oklahoma Panhandle in the Twentieth Century (Lubbock, Tex., 2006)

Also by Carolyn G. Hanneman

(with Robert B. Kamm and Carol L. Hiner) *The First Hundred Years: Oklahoma State University: People, Programs, Places* (Stillwater, Okla., 1990)

Milton Keynes UK
Ingram Content Group UK Ltd.
UKHW031458231024
450082UK00001B/62

9 780806 194936